Living as people of Hope

Living as people of

HOPE

by
Jeff Fountain

Hope for Europe

4

Living as people of Hope

© 2004 Jeff Fountain, Heerde
The author asserts the moral right to be identified as the author of this work.

Cover design: Maarten Nota, Lines communication & design, Gorinchem,
The Netherlands

Design and print: Lines communication & design, Gorinchem,
The Netherlands

Publisher: Initialmedia, Rotterdam, The Netherlands

The perspectives expressed in this book are those of the author and do not
necessarily reflect the positions of *Youth With A Mission* or *Hope for Europe.*

ISBN 90-74319-50-5

Initialmedia is a publisher of special interest books and magazines.

Books are published in close co-operation with writers and/or organizations.

*Sales and distribution of the published books are undertaken in close co-operation
with the writer and/or organizations through various channels.*

Initialmedia is an affiliate of Globalonline nv.

*Initialmedia bv - P.O. Box 21040 - 3001 AA Rotterdam - The Netherlands
E-mail: info@initialmedia.com * Internet: www.initialmedia.com .*

*For
Antonie & Gerinke
Stefan, Philip
& Jolien
and their generation,
the first to reach adulthood
in the new millennium*

*... and in memory
of Maartje
who found it difficult
to see God's hopeful future.*

6

With special thanks to:

Danica – without whom Part One never would have been written

Jelly – for her daily support in the office

Stuart & Gordon – together with whom I have been searching for Europe's hopeful future

Rob & Sarina – for a quiet place to write

Wyn & Shirley – for their example and encouragement all my life

& especially to

Romkje – my travelling companion through thick and thin on our journey towards God's future.

This is a book of grand themes
with practical and local application.
While addressing the European situation in the first place,
this book presents insights and proposes responses
relevant to much of the western world.
I write from personal experience in many countries
of Europe, but also against the background of daily life
in two rural Dutch towns, Heerde and Epe.
I attempt to link the spiritual and philosophical ideas
which have made Europe Europe,
and everyday developments and changes
happening under our noses,
echoed in many other parts of the world.
But primarily I attempt to offer reasons for hope
for the future of Europe, our lands
and our towns and cities.

Part One sketches the challenging situation of Europe
at the start of the new millennium.
Part Two responds to the question: how can we recover
faith, hope and vision for the future?

This book has questions after each chapter
for use in discussion groups.

Jeff Fountain

For I know the plans I have for you,
declares the LORD,
plans to prosper you and not to harm you,
plans to give you hope and a future.

Jeremiah 29:11

We have this hope
as an anchor for the soul,
firm and secure.
It enters the innner sanctuary behind the curtain,
where Jesus, who went before us,
has entered on our behalf

Hebrews 6: 19-20

CONTENTS

Part One: Six Questions

Part Two: Ten Imperatives

Part One
Six questions

*The challenging situation of Europe
at the start of the new millennium*

Prophecy is a tricky business,
especially when involving the future.
Chinese proverb

1. Who?

... dares predict

WE ALL REMEMBER where we were as midnight approached on December 31, 1999. The magical moment had finally come when, in an extravangant festival of fireworks and clinking glasses, we arrived safely in the new millennium!

But that transition was not without its tensions. Remember the Y2K scare? For months, even years, officials had warned us to prepare for shortages of power, food, money and fuel. Computer breakdowns, we were told, could cause anything from the failure of automated supermarket doors to planes falling out of the sky, or even accidental nuclear attacks.

Billboards set up by governmental agencies asked us: *'Are you ready for the new millennium? Is your company Y2K proof?'*

Computer firms had a boon selling new hardware. Many of us began storing extra food ... just in case.

To jog our short memories on how serious this situation appeared at the time, here are random excerpts from my e-mail files relating to this threat:

• *16 JUNE, 1999, USA:* Nearly half the American population considered it likely that people would panic and withdraw all their funds from the banks prior to year's end, a Gallup Poll concluded.

• Christian writer Gary North, one of the original voices warning of the impending Y2K debacle, commented: 'If this statistic does not produce damp shorts in the boardrooms of the New York banks, then the board members are brain-dead.'

• *26 JUNE 1999, GENEVA:* A UN agency has warned that a significant number of developing countries faced severe trade disruption and a collapse of customs operations at year's end because they were not ready to cope with the year 2000 problem. 'The consequences of inaction in this regard cannot be exaggerated,' said a senior official. 'There is a very serious risk that internal trade in a significant number of developing countries will be severely disrupted for an unpredictable number of weeks, maybe months,' he added.

• *8 JULY 1999, THE NETHERLANDS:* 'Now time is really running out.... Survey results indicate that disruptions in businesses, organisations and social processes are inevitable. Controlling these types of situations now deserves the highest priority!'

• *22 SEPTEMBER 1999, WASHINGTON DC, USA:* The Year 2000 computer glitch is likely to trigger international supply-chain disruptions that may end more than eight straight years of US economic growth, a Senate panel studying the problem said Wednesday. With 100 days left, the Special Committee on the Year 2000 Technology Problem said it was greatly concerned about the international Y2K picture for strategic as well as economic reasons. Severe long- and short-term disruptions to supply chains are likely to occur as a result of Y2K-related system failures, it said in its 288-page report.

The situation appeared indeed serious!

As an international mission organisation with operating locations in almost all European countries, we in YOUTH WITH A MISSION took these warnings seriously.

We sent out a Y2K check list to our leadership across the continent. We urged action to be taken to ensure Y2K compliancy both in our own office systems as well as those of our banks, suppliers and utility companies. We rescheduled training programmes to avoid the 'danger period', and developed contingency plans.

I wrote to our leaders across Europe:

> If we simply ignore the issue we can be guilty of executive negligence, failing to take necessary precautions. Even if we are convinced that the technical problem is grossly exaggerated, the wildcard is the social factor. How will people, especially Americans, react as we get closer to the end of the year? Will they withdraw investments in stocks en masse, causing a global stock market crash? Christians are often at the forefront of the alarmist lobby. David Wilkerson has circulated a prophetic scenario of the US army being called in to quell riots in Times Square, New York.
>
> In Europe there have been few signs of this panic factor. However, governments and industry have come to treat the problem with deadly seriousness. In Germany, the Hannover city power company conducted a public demonstration to show that all was under control. In great confidence the data-processing manager anticipated the approach of the midnight deadline, and then in horror watched the computer spew out thousands of error messages before freezing up entirely. For a few minutes it was impossible to monitor the electric grid or to trace equipment breakdowns. It took *seven months* to eradicate all the problems!
>
> The bottom line as I see it is that most western nations will suffer minor disruptions, while in central and eastern Europe, long power shortages are distinct possibilities.
>
> So please take the recommendations in this report seriously.

So... what did happen after the clocks ticked around to midnight?
Nothing!
NO-THING!!!!
AB-SO-LUTE-LY NOTHING!!!
Well, nothing significant. Maybe the odd glitch here and there. The Y2K doomsday predictions of global chaos failed spectacularly.
Phew!

Appropriate?
Perhaps this was an appropriate closure for a century fanfared by other famous predictions hopelessly wide of the mark.

• For, a hundred or so years ago, experts declared that radio had no future; that everything inventable had already been invented; that war would be fought only by machines; that flight by machines heavier-than-air was impractical and insignificant, if not impossible. And, of course, that the Titanic was unsinkable.

• The passing of the years saw more false prophecies. Atomic power? Pure fantasy! scoffed even Lord Rutherford, first to split the atom in the 1930's. Adolf Hitler boasted his Third Reich would last a thousand years. Erich Honecker declared the Berlin Wall would last a hundred years.

• World inflation would be history by 1959, predicted the International Monetary Fund. Guitar bands were on their way out, said the Decca Recording Company when turning down the Beatles in the early sixties. Even Bill Gates once mused that 640 kilobytes ought to be enough for anyone!

• Popular evangelical writers in the sixties and seventies predicted that communism would take over the world. My father's generation before that heard similar warnings about Mussolini and a revived Holy Roman Empire.

Surrounded by such a great cloud of false witnesses then, what dare *we* then say about the future?

What dare we say about tomorrow's Europe in this book?

Fools rush in where angels fear to tread, so let me predict the following three things to start with:

• One, no-one *really* knows what tomorrow's Europe will look like.

• Two, Europe tomorrow will not look like Europe today.

• Three, most predictions about tomorrow's Europe will also miss the mark.

But that should not stop us from asking ourselves what the future *could* hold for us in Europe.

In this book, we aim to pose and explore the following questions together:

- *Are we really ready for the new millennium? Are our churches ready to face the challenges of the new millennium?*
- *Who - and what ideas - will be the key shapers of tomorrow's Europe?*
- *What will happen if Christians remain passively on the sidelines, absorbed in their own church affairs?*
- *What might God's intentions be for Europe and Europeans in the twenty-first century?*
- *What could happen if God's people recovered vision for transformation in Europe?*
- *What could happen if we learnt to live as people of hope?*

For discussion:

- Where and how did you celebrate the new millennium?
- How seriously did you take the Y2K threat? Did you take any special precautions?
- What other false predictions can you think of?
- What is the value of asking what the future *could* look like?

II have always been a believer in Harry Truman's saying,
'Where there is no vision the people perish'.
Jean Monnet

2. Where?

... is the hope

AT THE WORLD EXHIBITION of 1900 in Paris, our great-grandparents could climb the giddy heights of the brand-new Eiffel Tower. From high above the great city they could gaze down on exhibits boasting the dazzling achievements of modern progress and scientific discovery.

Nothing seemed beyond human achievement. Science and reason were going to save the world. Confidence, optimism and expectation hung in the air.

But within a few short years–and a few short kilometres from the Eiffel itself–Europe's leading industrial nations would drag each other into the muddy trenches of the Somme and the Marne. The 'war to end all wars' summoned the harsh and bloody realities of the twentieth century.

One Depression, two World Wars and a Cold War later, little remains of our forefathers' naive optimism. Confident voices proclaiming a brave new world have been silenced by a resigned mood of cynicism and aimlessness. The global fascination with the 'Titanic' saga in the closing years of the twentieth century perhaps reflected widespread postmodern distrust in human pretensions of mastery over nature and destiny.

The last generation of last century was perhaps the first in recent times not to expect a better lifestyle than that of their parents. For them, the future 'just ain't what it used to be'.

New experiment
Yet something momentous and historic has been unfolding in Europe over the last half century, which also augurs a different future. Europe's borders have been melting before the advance of a radically new political experiment. The old order of sovereign nation states, dominant on the continent since Napoleon, has been giving way to a new reality increasingly affecting Europeans at all levels. In politics and business, crime prevention and sports, fishing and agriculture, ordinary Europeans everywhere wrestle with the day-to-day implications of the vision of a New Europe. Although part of the larger process of globalisation, the arrival of the Euro is one example of the all-pervasiveness of these new realities.

Already for years MTV watchers and European football fans have ignored national boundaries. Politicians, business executives and police have operated for decades across national borders, anticipating the implications of the new European realities. Mafia gangs operate networks of drugs, sex-slaves, illegal immigrants and black-money from Chechnya to Portugal...

Hope-bringers?
And we, followers of Jesus Christ, what is our vision for the New Europe? Yesterday's Europe was shaped significantly by Christian hope-bringers. So we would expect Christians to have a message of hope for tomorrow's Europe.

Surely we will be looking eagerly for signs of God's rule advancing among the European peoples in answer to our prayers for his Kingdom to come! After all, the Lord's Prayer implies a prayer for God's will to be done here *in Europe* as it is in heaven?!

Surely we will be in fervent dialogue with each other over a responsible, biblical attitude towards ever-increasing European union!?

Surely we will be seeking scriptural responses to potential threats to *shalom*[1] in tomorrow's Europe: nationalism, racism, urbanisation, pollution, illegal immigration, unemployment, the 'greying' of the population, sex-slavery, corruption in business and government, the wealth-poverty gap, the breakdown of values... !?

Surely we will be facing the future with faith, hope and expectancy, knowing how often the Spirit of God has broken into European history when all had seemed lost!? and knowing that Jesus Christ is the same, yesterday, today and forever!?

Surely....!?

The stark truth is this: at the dawn of the new millennium, there is all too little vision for tomorrow's Europe among God's people.

Where are today's prophetic voices with something from God to say about the New Europe?? Are we hearing enough from our pulpits to guide us towards the future in this continent? Why are there so few titles in the bookstores and libraries offering a biblical perspective on hope, or on the New Europe?[2]

Compromise
Leaders in all sorts of social, political and commercial sectors in European society today interact constantly across national borders. Yet Protestant church leaders by and large remain active only within the territories they inherited from the Reformation.

Medieval Europe was a mosaic glued together by the faith of a pan-European Roman Church. But the Reformation shattered that unity. Catholics and Protestants were divided along ethnic and linguistic lines. *'As the prince, so the religion'* was the compromise formulated in 1648 at the Treaty of Westphalia. The

1. *The Hebrew concept of Shalom is closely associated with the concept of the kingdom of God which we will address later. Meaning much more than simply 'peace', it refers to that state where everything is as God originally intended: right relationships, fulfilled purposes, proper functioning, etc*
2. *See Catherwood, Hume and Korthals Altes in the bibliography for titles that do address the New Europe.*

faith of the ruler would automatically be the official state faith. Hence the establishment of 'territorial' churches, state churches, married in a sense to the newly Protestant states.[3]

Today as the borders dissolve between member states of the European Union, we have become conscious of a further effect of this compromise Unlike the Roman Catholic Church, Europe's Protestant churches are largely tied to their own formerly-sovereign territories, and have few direct relationships with the churches of other nations. This is also true of younger evangelical and pentecostal denominations whose vision is too often limited to their own nation.

Few evangelical leaders seem to be addressing the new realities of Europe. We seem to have little to say about the New Europe. We seem to have little faith for God's Kingdom to come in any greater measure in Europe, for His will to be done in Europe.

There simply appears to be little vision for tomorrow's Europe. One of the fathers of the European Union, Jean Monnet, once said: 'I have always been a believer in Harry Truman's saying, "Where there is no vision the people perish".'(!)

Monnet obviously didn't know his Bible. Those who do will recognise Truman's 'wisdom' as one of Solomon's ancient proverbs: chapter 29, verse 18.

But Monnet, a 'free thinker', *did* have vision for Europe.

What about those of us who think we know our Bibles? What is *our* vision for tomorrow's Europe?

Today across Europe, the church in many places is 'perishing'. King Solomon (and President Truman) could tell us why.

We lack vision.

---

3. *One can only speculate as to the spiritual dimension of this development, but perhaps a compromise was made here to territorial spiritual powers. This compromise meant that national churches in each Protestant land had a close 'chaplaincy' role to the throne, rather than a prophetic one, and no evangelistic involvement in other lands. As in England today, the ruler was the official defender of the faith, and therefore in a Protestant land was not permitted to be Catholic. It was not the duty of believers in one land to be involved in evangelism and mission in another, whose spiritual protector was the ruler of that land. This territorialism was a major reason why, for 300 years after the Reformation, Protestants showed little initiative in foreign missions.*

Good news, bad news

Yet God's people are always called to be people of hope. We have been entrusted with a message of hope. We have good news to tell about Jesus Christ and God's rule. It's a message of hope for individuals, for families, for whole communities, for nations - even for lifespheres.

In fact, it's a message of hope for the whole cosmos! The Bible reveals how one day *everything* under heaven and earth will be reconciled under Christ's lordship. *Everything!!* Sacred *and* secular.[4]

But the good news begins with bad news. The human race has a terminal heart condition. The heart of the human problem remains the problem of the human heart. Aleksandr Solzhenitsyn, the Russian dissident and author, came to this realisation in his prison cell in the gulag: *the line between good and evil does not run between nations and ideologies, but through every human heart.*[5]

Only accurate diagnosis of the human condition can lead to effective treatment. Only the gospel diagnoses this problem accurately. Remedies based on any other diagnosis are mere quackery.

Only the gospel has the remedy for Europe's (and the world's) root problem of sin, which surfaces in countless social, economic and political problems. Think of the cost to society of extra housing for broken families, of rising crime levels, of drug and alcohol abuse, of sexual violence, of corruption in Europe's governmental circles, of UN peacekeeping in Bosnia and Kosovo, of the widespread ecological disasters in Russia stemming indirectly from an atheistic worldview... etcetera, etcetera.

Even before death, the wages of sin are pretty costly!

The good news is that God has already done something about this terminal condition. Sin and its consequence, death, have been legally dealt with through the death and resurrection of his sinless son, Jesus Christ. Reconciliation and restoration are now

---

4 *See Romans 8:19-21; Colossians 1:15-20*
5. *See The Gulag Archipeligo, vol 2, in the chapter entitled "The Ascent of the Soul"*

possible. We *can* be reconciled to our Maker, to our neighbour, to our environment. We *can* be restored to God's original purposes for us as individuals, as families and communities, as peoples and as the human race. Good news indeed!

When God's people have faithfully lived and shared this message, major social changes have occurred in Europe. Individuals and families have changed. Warring tribes and nations have been reconciled. Security, social harmony and meaningful lifestyles have resulted. Whole communities and people groups have come to view life with new hope and expectation.

This–and none other–is the message that has taught the human race to hope, as we shall see later.

Where is the hope?
Yet when God's people have lost vision and hope, the Church's influence has perished. The light has lost its brightness. The salt has lost its saltiness.[6] In the eyes of the world, the Church has become irrelevant. God's people have become spectators, not players. And the credibility of the people of hope has suffered.

Today people the world over need hope. *Faith* may well be considered irrelevant and old-fashioned by many of our contemporaries. *Love* may well have been reduced to sex in our self-obsessed culture. But the one who offers *hope* leads.

Despite the recent overthrow of dictators and the passing of the Cold War, millions of our fellow Europeans still face empty and uncertain futures. Whoever offers them hope will lead - whether or not that hope is based on truth. Hitler offered hope to a defeated German people in the 1930's, and won the leader-ship.

Do we, people of God, have hope to offer our fellow Europeans? If so, why do they not look to *us* for direction? Why do they so often conclude that the Christian message is irrelevant? that the Church belongs to the past, not to the future? that Christians have nothing relevant to say about the headline

---

6. *See Matthew 5:13-16*

issues of today?

Let's put ourselves in their shoes for a moment. When thoughtful, non-church-going Europeans look at us, the Church, what do they see? When they listen to our message, spoken and acted, what do they hear?

Too often they see us retreating into the comfort zones of our congregations, playing spiritual parlour games among ourselves, the 'sacred' parts of our lives divorced from the 'secular' parts.

Message heard: Christians have little hope to offer tomorrow's Europe.

Too often they see us absorbed with our doctrinal disagreements over a gospel apparently irrelevant to the everyday concerns of business people, politicians, factory-workers, the young and the unemployed.

Message heard: Christians have little hope to offer tomorrow's Europe.

Too often they hear an expectation that things have to get worse and worse–an eschatology of 'gloom and doom'–and that all attempts towards European unity are antichrist conspiracies.

Message heard: Christians have little hope to offer tomorrow's Europe.

Too often they see a hopelessly 'balkanised' Church, desperately weak in pan-European relationships, unable to demonstrate unity in diversity, and lacking the moral authority to lead the nations of Europe in their quest for unity.

Message heard: Christians have little hope to offer tomorrow's Europe.

Too often they see us as living in the past, and our expressions of corporate worship as quaint relics of bygone times. They look at the Orthodox church and glimpse Byzantium. The Church of Rome reminds them of medievalism. The traditions and vestments of some traditional protestant clergy can conjure up the sixteenth or seventeenth centuries. Some non-conformist evangelical services still reflect elements of the nineteenth century, while pentecostal meetings may evoke nostalgia for the early twentieth century...

Message heard: Christians have little hope to offer tomorrow's Europe.

This may not all be fair.

But, let's be honest. Some of it is.

Many of our contemporaries see and hear us through these

filters. Little wonder they do not look to us for answers to Europe's problems! Little wonder they do not regard us as being people of hope! Little wonder the Church of Jesus Christ has lost her leadership role in Europe! Little wonder we are perishing with-out vision in Europe!

In the language of Deuteronomy, *we have become the tail and not the head.*[7]

Ten imperatives
Hope requires a vision of the future. Without expectation there is no hope. If our expectation level is low, we hardly qualify as people of hope.

How then *can* we recover vision, hope and expectation for Europe? How do we become the 'head' once more, leading the nations towards God's purposes?

By walking together through the following 'ten imperatives for God's people', perhaps we can begin to recover biblical hope for Europe in the twenty-first century.

• Firstly, we need to **ask** what God's will is for Europe.
Is it really God's will that his will would not be done in Europe, as some 'end-time' prophets seem to imply?

• Secondly, we should **reject** the enemy's disinformation.
Our adversary is the master propagandist, and we have believed too much of his disinformation about the permanency of Marxism, Islam, secular humanism, and other -isms.

• Thirdly, we must **recognise** what God has done in the past.
He has invested uniquely in the European peoples over twenty centuries, and still expects a return on his investment.

• Fourthly, we should **admit** honestly past sins and mistakes of

---

7. *See Deut. ch.28:13,44 The use of the word 'head' is not meant here in the sense of dominating society through political power, as happened all too often in Christendom; rather it means leadership through servanthood.*

the people of God.

Many of today's headlines in Europe today stem directly or indirectly from the failures of God's people in the past. What must we do about this today?

- Fifthly, we need to **look** at what God is up to!

The shaking of the Marxist world over the past decade is just one of a number of indicators that the Lord of history still has purposes for the European peoples. Expect the surprises of God!

- Sixthly, we have to **face up** to the truth about the present.

'Christian' Europe of all continents is particularly guilty of deliberately suppressing the knowledge of God, and has become a desperately needy mission field.

- Seventhly, we must **rediscover** the gospel of the Kingdom.

The good news about the reconciliation of all things, through Christ's work on the cross, applies to every sphere of life affected by sin: family life, church life, governmental affairs, business and economics, education, arts and entertainment, law and health, sports and so on.

- Eighthly, we ought to **embrace** our responsibility and role to be salt and light in our world.

Only the church of Jesus Christ has the adequate message and authority to stand against tyranny. It's time to exchange our minority complex for a 'creative minority' complex.

- Ninthly, we need to **transplant** the church into the cultures of the twenty-first century.

To survive the transition into the new millennium, and to appeal to the younger generations, we must encourage radical experimentation in the search for new relevant wineskins.

- Lastly, it is imperative that we **synergise!**

God does not give the full picture to any one group or denomination or stream; in order to regain full vision, we need to be in proper relationship with other parts of the Body of Christ, learning to partner together towards the building of the Kingdom - locally, nationally and throughout the continent.

Ten imperatives! We will take a closer look at these imperatives in Part Two of this book.

Options
However, before we examine these ten imperatives more closely, let's first consider Europe's future options.

Tomorrow's Europe will be shaped by the basic beliefs of tomorrow's Europeans. Max Weber's dictum, *'ideas have consequences'*, implies that lifestyle flows out of worldview. Our ideas about ultimate reality, about God, nature, the supernatural, human personhood, our origins and the afterlife, all shape our lifestyle, our priorities, our values, our morals and our relationships.

In our extraordinary age of rapid change, futurology has become a major industry. Futurologists rightly warn us that 'either we take hold of the future, or the future will take hold of us'.[8] Trends and technological developments are analysed to form an educated best guess at the future, for businesses and governments to plan by.

The think tank of the European Commission in Brussels, the *Forward Studies Unit*, has produced a most stimulating working paper entitled, *Scenarios Europe 2010: Five possible futures for Europe*.[9] Its purpose was not to try to predict what *will* actually happen in the year 2010. Rather it sketched varying scenarios based on certain factors and developments being more dominant than others, to offer a range of feasible possibilities. The intention was to foster a 'future culture' within the EU, a forward looking approach (something we in our churches and organisations could learn from).

---

8. See Dixon, *Futurewise*
9. *http://www.hfe.org/resources/article list.php*

The five scenarios were entitled:

• *Triumphant markets*: the triumph of trade over war, the American way favouring entrepreneurship and quick profits, where the 'user pays', ushers in the long-heralded Third Industrial Revolution globally.

• *A hundred flowers*: a decentralised participative democracy where governments and mulitnationals have little decisive influence after losing their moral legitimacy early in the new century.

• *Shared responsibilities:* where political authorities partner with firms, individuals and civic associations to assume their share of the life of the broader community.

• *Creative societies:* in which reforms have returned man to his rightful place at the heart of economic development and laying foundations for a new social solidarity stressing quality of life, and rejecting materialism and obsession with productivity.

• *Turbulent neighbourhoods*: instable political situations in countries surrounding Europe have created a preoccupation with security at the expense of domestic issues; globalisation has increased weath disparity rather than increased general wealth; organised crime, arms-dealing and terrorism contribute to a creeping anarchy from the borders of Europe.

What is noticeable is the absence of the church in shaping any of these futures - despite the fact that I know several of those involved in the think tank to be devout believers.

Unspoken are the basic wordviews behind the various ideologies shaping these scenarios. But I wonder if there is not a fundamental shift happening in what Europeans believe - that could lead us down another path...

What belief systems *could* shape tomorrow's Europe? In broad categories, the options are surprisingly few. In fact, we Europeans have already dabbled in virtually all of them. What are these options? And how have they shaped Europe over the past 2000 years? What options are we Europeans likely to choose for the immediate future? What sort of Europe could result from these options?

Bizarre
While travelling to the Balkans in the summer of 1999, I had a bizarre and provocative encounter with a woman whose worldview was very different from my own. Frankly, she 'rattled my cage'.

And in so doing, she opened my eyes to realise that our journey towards tomorrow's Europe may well be a turbulent ride - *back* to the future.   ↙

For discussion:

- With how much of this chapter do you agree/disagree?
- *We have become the tail and not the head'.* How true is this in your experience?
- How do non-Christians you know view Christians and the Church?
- *'Hope requires a vision of the future. Without expectation there is no hope'.* What future vision for Europe do most Christians you know share?

When a man ceases to believe in God,
he doesn't believe in nothing;
he believes in anything.
G.K.Chesterton

3. What?

... is happening here

DANICA AND I FOUND OURSELVES stranded together in the bustling airport lounge in Budapest, capital of Hungary. We were both flying to Sarajevo, but our delayed flight from Amsterdam had missed its connection.

While airline personnel worked on a solution for our ongoing travel, we sat in the lounge's grey plastic bucket seats and commiserated on our predicament.

I was en route to teach in our first YWAM Discipleship Training School in Bosnia, a country which was struggling to resume some sort of normalcy after four ravaging years.

Danica explained she was a psychotherapist, and planned to spend three weeks in a war-forlorn Bosnian town conducting therapy groups among women who had been raped and whose menfolk had been maimed or killed.

This practical expression of reconciliation therapy intrigued me. I wanted to hear more. I explained I worked for a Christian mission also involved in reconciliation work in Bosnia and elsewhere.

She quietly outlined her concept of the therapy circle to me.

'I call it a *kolo* - that's an ancient Bosnian word which resonates in their spirits,' she explained.

'We're sorry,' broke in the girl behind the desk, 'but we can't get you a flight to Sarajevo until the day after tomorrow. We'll have to put you up in a hotel here in Budapest.'

Groaning inwardly, I thought of the disruption to the school's programme in Sarajevo. And of forty-eight unplanned hours in Budapest. Well, I could look up my colleagues in the city...

Danica seemed to take the setback calmly and philosophically. 'I just go with the flow,' she smiled. 'This was meant to be.'

We continued our discussion as the airport minibus took us into the city and wound its way through the narrow streets lined with newly-renovated historic facades. Eventually we were dropped off at a downtown hotel. As we went off to our rooms, Danica suggested we continue talking about our interests in Bosnia over a meal in the hotel dining hall.

Hot spots
So under a high-vaulted ceiling and over the quiet clatter of cutlery, Danica explained that while her parents were Bosnian Serbs, she had grown up and studied in America and lived for a while in Europe. She was now in her mid-forties, married, and with two teen-aged children. She was a forensic counsellor for US law courts, had worked for both the UN and the EU. She counselled anorexia patients and rape victims, and held workshops and seminars in universities, churches and other institutions.

However, when she handed me her card, with the line 'integrating Feminist Archetypal Psychology with an holistic scholarship', I felt the first inklings that perhaps I was getting into something over my head. On the flip-side were listed a number of conferences and tours she was conducting to ancient European archaeological sites, including the world's oldest human constructions in Malta, and the labyrinth of Knossos on Crete. I had a vague concept of a labyrinth as a subterranean maze of passages, but what it stood for in antiquity, I had no clue.

'You know, don't you, that these ancient ruins on Malta

predate the pyramids?'

Actually, I didn't.

Enthusiastically she went on to tell me about the matriarchal society of pre-Christian Europe, Old Europe, as she called it. Old Europeans worshipped the Mother Goddess. Free from gender-bias, these societies enjoyed a golden age of peace. But then along came the sky gods of the bronze age–including the Jewish-Christian God–and the patriarchal age of violence and gender-suppression began...

Racing through the files of my mind I tried to remember details about pre-Christian Europe. The classical period hadn't really interested me as a student on the other side of the world in New Zealand where I grew up. I was, however, more familiar with the Celtic and Germanic societies the first Christian messengers had encountered: dominated by fear of unpredictable gods and spirits, my memory told me. But I didn't recall learning about any Golden Age in my history studies at university.

Now Danica was telling me how the Celtic burial mounds found across Europe represented the womb of the Earth Goddess. These I did know of, as my wife Romkje and I had come across examples three or four thousand years old on walks in the countryside in central Holland where we live.

'Bodies were ceremonially carried into the long entrance passage, you know, the vaginal passage,' she explained matter-of-factly, 'and implanted in the burial chamber–the uterus–ready for reincarnation.'

This woman was not exactly inhibited, I noted to myself, talking to a stranger like me.

These Old European societies, she continued, had deep spiritual insights about reality which had been smothered by the later patriarchal eras. Without modern science or technology, for example, the ancients had divined the exact locations of sacred centres, spiritual 'hot-spots' or dimensional gateways to the other-world. Sacred centres provided spiritual direction and orientation in Old Europe and beyond, she patiently explained to her new pupil.

I looked again at the business card in my hand. Also listed was a trip to ancient Celtic sites in Ireland, staying at the Inn of the Hill of the Witch. I glanced up at the woman sitting opposite me. Could she herself be a modern-day witch? Urbane, articulate, sophisticated, well-read and self-assured, she was deadly serious about everything she was telling me. What sort of woman was she? What sort of mystic, fringe movement did she represent? What did her esoteric collection of finger-rings mean?

And what I was doing listening to this gobble-de-gook?! Maybe I should politely excuse myself from this conversation, I wondered. I was out of familiar territory and should play safe. This woman was challenging some of my deepest beliefs about God and reality. Besides, evangelical mission leaders didn't usually meet in hotels with 'pagan, Jungian, feminist, archetypal psychotherapists' (her own description), did they?

Run away?! What was I afraid of? Discovering that 'God' really was just a bronze-age sky god, after all? That what I had built my life on was an illusion, a bronze-age myth?

Unchartered

Many years ago as a student I had gone through a serious faith struggle. I had then committed myself to honest pursuit of truth. I should not fear confrontation with other worldviews. That should keep me honest.

Francis Schaeffer used to say, the truth of Christianity is that it is true to what is there. 'You can go to the end of the world,' he once wrote, 'and you never need to be afraid, like the ancients, that you will fall off the end and the dragons will eat you up.' [10]

If God was not who the Bible claimed him to be, then Christianity was a sham and I wanted no part in it. But if he *was* who the Bible claimed him to be, then he commanded my total allegiance. He was either Lord of all, or not Lord at all.

Danica's challenges required honest responses. But I had no ready response. These were unchartered waters for me. She was the first devout pagan packaged as a civilised, sophisticated

---

10. *He is there and he is not silent, Schaeffer, p17*

westerner with whom I could remember having a conversation. Not pagan in the sense of atheistic, simply not believing in God; but pagan in the sense of actively embracing the deities of polytheism, animism and spiritism. These were -ism's I associated with dead, ancient civilisations, or primitive tribes far away in Africa or New Guinea. Not with cosmopolitan contemporaries here in the West.

For Danica the word 'pagan' held positive connotations – 'no, not barbarian!' she corrected me firmly on one occasion. For her, the word 'Christian' held the same pejorative overtones as 'pagan' did for me. She equated the Old European paganism with a peaceful, matriarchal society - more civilised in many respects than our own.

History had been my university major, and for over twenty years I had taught the story of Christian missions against a backdrop of European history. But for me, the real story had only started four thousand years ago with Abraham.

Danica was now exposing my ignorance of pre-Christian European life. The biblical record, I realised, only offered eleven telescoped chapters on pre-Abrahamic history as introduction to the story of redemption. That was all I had cared to know about.

Until now.

Danica had simply dismissed the Judaic-Christian God as a bronze-age innovation. How should I respond?

I tried to start from historical ground I knew.

'Danica, who do you think Jesus of Nazareth was?'

'There you go,' she smiled indulgently, 'with your patriarchal, "either-or" thinking.' Side-stepping the question, she added, 'You Christians need to learn to think out of the box, and not just in black-and-white, either-or, right-or-wrong categories.'

Oh.

I had just run into the disdain mystics have for history and the idea that historical happenings can reveal eternal truths. History seemed to offer few grounds for dialogue.

Ill-equipped

At one point in the conversation, Danica leaned across the table and asked–in rather colourful language–if the Christian God, the Ultimate Patriarch really was male. Surely masculine titles like 'Lord', 'King', 'Father' alienated the female majority of the world's population, she suggested.

This typical feminist line was not so new. I could give tidy mental answers to this charge: Genesis 1:26 described God as having created humankind in 'his' image, male and female. So of course God was more than just male.

Yet somehow Danica's question hit me with new force. 'She's right!' I thought. 'I *do* have an anthropomorphic perception of God as a male.'

Obviously God had created gender and therefore was gender-transcendent. The divine image in humans was expressed in complementary sexuality, male *and* female. And yet we talked about the divine in gender-bound language, preferring *He* to *She* or *It*. Yes, Jesus taught us to call God 'Father', but was this not a statement about intimate relationship rather than a gender statement?

Again my preconceptions were being challenged. I was being forced to recognise serious cultural baggage in my perceptions of biblical truth - by a woman who called herself a pagan, a worshipper of the Mother Goddess!

As our conversation continued on from the one subject to another, I felt I was being led on a grand tour to look at life and reality through a completely new set of eyes, 'unencumbered' by a lifetime of Christian teaching and influence. At the same time, I felt naive, clumsy and ignorant, unable to build an effective communication bridge into her world.

I was used to giving answers. But now I had to listen and learn: about how pagans viewed the world, including Christianity, and about how ill-equipped I was to share the good news of God's shalom with a contemporary pagan.

Familiar
Later as I returned to my room, questions swirled in my mind. What was happening here? Was this a diabolical trap? Was I being bewitched? Or could it be a divine set-up? Could God

somehow be in this encounter? Was this indeed 'meant to be', as Danica had mused at the airport? If so, by whom, or what?

By now I was supposed to be in Sarajevo. Instead I was booked for two nights into the same Budapest hotel as a woman who could have stepped out of the pages of a Harry Potter novel, from a world–or worlds–unfamiliar to me. If men were from Mars and women from Venus, Danica seemed to be from Pluto!

As I lay on my bed, I traced a mental map of our conversation covering subjects we ranged over and questions raised - a map I would later reproduce on paper in Sarajevo.

We were poles apart in worldviews. Yet something about Danica's perspective resonated. What was it? Unlike so many Europeans, Danica strongly affirmed the spiritual realm, and was not impressed with the pursuit of the western materialistic dream. That in itself was refreshing. We shared a common understanding of the *reality* of the spiritual - if not a common understanding of the *truth* about that realm.

She was concerned about the environment, about realising one's full potential, about peace and justice, about the balance between being and doing, about gender issues - questions that ought to concern biblical Christians. She even seemed to talk my language about faith and finances! 'Isn't it amazing how the money just seems to come in when you need to do a project - like this trip of mine to Bosnia?' she had exclaimed to my surprise, as if expecting me to fully understand.

Yes, we shared many areas of common concern. But her experience, especially with her Serbian Orthodox upbringing and also her impression of American evangelicalism, had led her to view the Church as a major part of the problem.

Her vision for a New Europe would be a revived Old Europe. Old, animistic, pagan Europe - in a new sophisticated form.

That was a disturbing–yet vaguely familiar–thought...

For discussion:

- *Have you ever met anyone who seriously called themselves 'pagan'?*
- *If so, what was your response then? Could you find a communication bridge with that person?*
- *How would you have reacted to Danica?*
- *Are you familiar with the pre-Christian beliefs Danica talked about?*

History repeats itself.
Has to.
Nobody listens.
Steve Turner

4. How?

... do we get out of here

SLEEP DID NOT COME EASILY. I tossed and turned on my hotel bed, a hundred and one questions tumbling through my mind.

I switched on the bedside lamp and distractedly picked up the tourist magazine laying by the bed. The words on the cover jumped off the page at me.

'Visit the labyrinth of Buda Castle.'

Labyrinth?!!

Danica had talked about a labyrinth in Knossos, on Crete. And there was one right here in Budapest?!

Sleep was definitely a hundred miles away now. This was really weird! And a little creepy. Until today I had never talked to anyone in my life about labyrinths, and here next to my bed was an article about a labyrinth just a few minutes' walk away! I had been to Budapest many times before, and had never heard of any labyrinth. Was my encounter with Danica opening my eyes to things I just didn't have eyes for before?

So what really was a labyrinth? And where did it fit in Danica's world? The article explained a labyrinth to be a 'preliterate philosophical and poetic statement' about the web of paths through life and reality. This particular labyrinth, however, was a complex of caves and passages formed by hot water springs underneath Castle Hill, on the Buda side of the Danube River.

An interesting footnote was that there in these bewildering corridors, German ss troops had taken their last stand against the conquering Red Army late in World War Two. The Russians had then used it as a secret military installation during the Cold War.

Recently restored to its pre-war condition, the labyrinth was now open to the public and offered *'the opportunity to explore Hungary's mythic and spiritual past, and perhaps discover the silver thread that would lead you through your own personal labyrinth.'*

Silver thread? My knowledge of the classics failed me once more. I was yet to become familiar with the ancient legend of the labyrinth at Knossos in Crete, where King Minos sacrificed Athenian maidens and youths by sending them into the labyrinth where they would meet the deadly Minotaur (Minos-bull). Minos' daughter, Ariadne, mentioned in the magazine article, saved the young hero Theseus, by giving him a ball of silver thread which he unwound as he entered the labyrinth. After slaying the Minotaur, Theseus simply retraced the thread to find his way out.

Next morning, Danica's surprise was almost as great as mine had been when I showed her the article. She had never been to Budapest before, and so readily agreed to my suggestion to visit the Labyrinth of Buda Castle in the mid-afternoon.

Meanwhile, I was glad for the chance to meet with my fellow YWAMers, and to talk and pray with them about this woman who was getting under my skin! I felt I was on a steep learning curve about spiritual realities that had shaped–and were still shaping–Europe.

I was in for more lessons that afternoon.

Journey
Perspiration from the mid-summer's heat trickled down my face as I climbed up the hill from the Danube. The brightly patterned

tiled roof of St Mathias Cathedral dominated the skyline on top of Castle Hill ahead.

Danica was already waiting by the labyrinth entrance. My apprehension of the unknown was not exactly soothed when she sniggered under her breath, 'What will my colleagues say when I tell them I visited a labyrinth with a Christian *minister?!*' What was that supposed to mean? What sort of colleagues did she have?

We descended the stone stairway into a comfortably cool reception area, paid the entrance fee and received a guidesheet with a map of the labyrinth. I joked nervously with the receptionist, asking if everyone who had gone in had come out again.

We studied the guidesheet and the map before heading off into the dimly-lit passage formed by rough-hewn rock walls about two metres apart.

Soon the passage widened into a chamber with a stone table and bench. Off to the left was another chamber, with what seemed to be a large drain pipe suspended from the ceiling directly over a similar pipe protruding out of the ground. A pale blue light shone in both segments and a throbbing heart-beat sound pulsated in the chamber. On the ground around the pipe were indicated the cardinal points of the compass. If I could believe my information guide, what we beheld before us was nothing less than 'the Axis of the World, the centre or origin of the world'!

Eureka! I thought cynically, just what I had been looking for all my life: two drain pipes claiming to be the origin of the world. That explained something about our poor, polluted planet, I mused.

I read on in my guidesheet: *The tree of the world, the Menhir, the shaman tree, the obelisk, the tree of life - all these are various manifestations of the Axis of the World, designating the Middle of the World and providing a point of orientation in the labyrinthine maze of space. These sacred centres...*

Wait a minute! Sacred centres... Danica had talked about these last night. I had dismissed it as 'gobble-de-gook'. And without her or me then knowing anything about the existence of this place, here we were now staring at the 'real' thing.[11] What powers had engineered this *synchronicity*, as Carl Jung would have called such a coincidence?

Befuddled, I motioned to Danica to sit with me at the stone table, and asked her to explain more about the concept of the labyrinth. I had obviously missed something in my education and was now on a crash course in pre-Christian spiritual history of Europe.

Like the Celtic burial-mounds, she explained patiently, labyrinths represented the womb of the Earth Mother. Labyrinths were originally burial sites, with an elaborate system of passages to ward off grave robbers.[12] The labyrinth was a place of darkness, death and rebirth, a place of sacrifice, transformation and reincarnation, she explained. It was a place to confront and conquer the minotaurs in your own life. It could also be a symbolic journey into the Other-world, she added.

The Other-world?! Light began to dawn. Dimensional gateways! Like in the movies. *Stargate. Star Trek. Star Wars. The X-Files. The Matrix!* Yes, of course, that was all a familiar concept to today's youth, moving in and out of dimensions, back and forth into other worlds, time warps, transformations. 'Beam me up, Scotty', and all that.

Seeing *The Matrix* for the first time with my youngest teenaged son, Philip, a few days before leaving on this trip, had made me feel very middle-aged. I had been tuned in just enough to realise I was missing so much of the layers of metaphor and imagery.

---

11. *Whether this labyrinth and the Axis of the world were authentic ancient sites, or simply a contemporary adaptation of subterranean passages that resembled an ancient labyrinth, was not clear at first from the literature. Neither was that so important for me. The fact that the Buda Castle labyrinth had been 'resurrected' at great cost to some government department meant that Danica was not alone in her fascination with Old Europe.*
12. *Knossos had been incorrectly assumed to be an inhabited palace, I later read, but its construction was more like that of a movie set, with fake urns, fake furnishings, fake plumbing, fake floor-tiles. It was actually a lavish tomb for King Minos. The word 'labyrinth' derived from the Greek word labrys, a two-headed axe, the design found on furnishings in Minos' tomb.*

But now it became obvious: the telephone booth in *The Matrix* was a dimensional gateway, something like this Sacred Centre. Characters in the film–Morpheus, Trinity, Neo–returned to the other dimension, often just in the nick of time, through the telephone booth.

Youth would have no problem relating to the concept of the Other-world. Their fantasies had already been attuned to it by a generation of films.

Parallels

On through passages resembling sets for *Raiders of the Lost Ark* we continued; past the closed entrance to the Personal Labyrinth, where those 'not afraid of themselves' could enter at night by appointment, the guidesheet informed us, in the search for the self. Obviously Danica had fellow-travellers here in Budapest on the same journey back to Old Europe.

A series of replicas of prehistoric cave drawings, mainly from the famous Lascaux caves in France, enticed us into the Prehistoric Labyrinth. Bulls, symbol of fertility and divinity, featured prominently, and were, according to the guide, radiant with the 'eternal harmony of prehistoric times'. Hints of the Golden Age again.

We passed on into a darker chamber where, I read, *gloomier paintings and carvings, wrought with tension, indicate the dissolution of primordial harmony: the occurrence of violent death, of possessiveness, of pain and suffering... Along with the loss of harmony there is nevertheless a feeling of yearning, for the re-establishment of the accord between Man and Nature, now out of tune: it is this yearning which manifests itself in the figure of the magician or shaman of Les Trois, on the rock standing in the middle of the hall.*

Here were clear parallels with the biblical account of Eden and the Fall. A sacrificial stone revealed an innate awareness of the need for shed blood to appease the spiritual powers Perhaps, I mused, there were more communication bridges between the biblical and pagan worldviews, than with the materialist worldview. The materialist would have had no use for a sacrificial stone.

Another figure of a shaman wearing a wolf skin and a deer-mask welcomed us into the section labelled The Labyrinth of History. The shaman was spiritual leader, priest, teacher, soothsayer and healer. He stood next to a shaman tree, pointing both to heaven and to the underworld. Superhuman efforts climbing up and down the shaman tree on symbolic journeys to the Other-world gave special knowledge to the shaman. The dimensional gateway concept again.

The reference to descending to the underworld triggered an almost heretical thought. Did not one of the messianic psalms say Jesus descended into hades to set captives free? Could not Jesus then be described as the perfect shaman figure - the go-between for this world, the underworld and the heavens?

We continued on down the passageways and through the centuries; past the Magic Deer that according to legend had led the nomadic Magyars westward from Asia; on to the mythical sword of Attila the Hun.

Danica was in her element. 'They've done this so well! I couldn't have designed it any better myself,' she exclaimed. This was her world - a world much bigger than I had first understood.

She clearly identified with these polytheistic, animistic pre-Christian Europeans. They were part of her Old Europe, and believed the physical or natural world to be 'animated' by the spiritual or supernatural world, as a hand might 'animate' a glove.[13] The Greek, Roman, Germanic, Celtic, Nordic and Slavic worldviews were all animistic. Animism–in its broadest sense–was Europe's earliest belief system.

Satirical
Unexpectedly, we next came across a large baptismal font. It represented a clear discontinuity with what we had seen so far. We seemed to be moving now from Danica's world towards my own. For phase depicted here was when the Magyars embraced monotheism and rejected paganism - at least, outwardly. This

---

13. *From the Latin word 'anima' meaning 'breath' or 'soul'.*

Christianisation of the Magyars, their first major shift in worldview, was symbolised by the crowning of St Stephen at Christmas, AD1000.

A further corridor lined by Mongol figurines depicted the brief threat posed by Genghis Khan and the Tartar invasion, before opening into a large ivy-decked chamber. In the centre stood a fountain perpetually spouting wine, recalling the chivalrous fifteenth century era of the Hungarian kings and the Holy Roman Empire.

A large crowned head half-buried in the ground portrayed the demise of the Hungarian kingdom, and the start of the Ottoman occupation. The Moslem Turks represented yet another form of monotheism, one Hungary suffered but never embraced.

The guidesheet concluded with the comment that since then and until 1989, Hungary had been mostly under foreign rulers, the most recent being the Russians. Soviet rule of course had attempted to suppress the Church, imposing its own marxist brand of materialism.

This was not the only expression of materialism that had signalled the second major worldview shift - as the next section of the labyrinth reminded us. A puzzling inscription described the discovery of extinct humanoid fossils in the hills around Budapest. Eventually we realised it was a satirical comment on the modern era of so-called *homo consumus!*

Clay imprints of a Nike shoe, a skeleton grasping a Coke can and a computer keyboard provided a tongue-in-cheek reminder that Europeans today were again at a crossroads, this time rejecting materialism as a world view.

Metaphor
Our walk through the labyrinth had taken us on a journey through history from *animism* to *theism* and eventually to a cynical look at *materialism*. By now, I was awakening to the realisation that, for the first time ever in history, European thinkers had tried, and spurned, all three options in turn. What other options remained? Where could they turn to now?

Earlier in the labyrinth, as we came to a junction of several corridors, we had met a group of schoolgirls looking lost and disorientated. Almost pouncing on us, they had asked half desperately, "How do we exit from here?"

With no map it was indeed most confusing to know which path to take. We had had to consult our guidesheet constantly to find our way out of loops and dead ends thus far. So after further examination of our map, we had sent them off in the right direction towards the exit.

What was it I had read in the tourist magazine the night before? Something about the labyrinth being a 'pre-literate philosophical and poetic statement' about the web of paths through life and reality?

What a metaphor for Europe's search for truth and meaning through the centuries! Now having rejected the possibility of there being any true map of reality at all, postmodern Europeans were as lost and confused in history's maze as these schoolgirls without a map.

Pilgrimage

We were nearly back to the reception area where we began. There was one last display area, which added yet another twist to the story of the labyrinth. Ancient-looking prints exhibited in a row of glass cases drew me closer for inspection. These were samples of beautifully calligraphed labyrinths, the painstaking work of generations of monks. One depicted the whole gospel of John written in minuscule letters following meandering paths through a labyrinthine pattern.

Obviously at some stage the Church had 'baptised' the pagan imagery of the labyrinth. Yes, explained Danica, one famous labyrinth was in Chartres Cathedral in France. She often used that labyrinth design in her own workshops, she added, helping people to respond to the dead ends of life, like divorces and illnesses.

Later I learnt that in troubled times when pilgrimages were too dangerous, tiled labyrinth designs on cathedral floors became popular substitutes as devotional exercises. Despite its pagan roots, the labyrinth as a metaphor of life's twists and turns became a meditation aid in many a monastery garden, with hedges creating a maze form, often with a water fountain in the centre.

Danica's description of the labyrinth as a place of darkness, death and rebirth, a place of sacrifice, transformation and reincarnation, had been infused with new Christian connotations, resurrection replacing reincarnation. Thus Theseus' escape from death in the labyrinth of Knossus was paralleled by Jesus' resurrection from the tomb in Jerusalem.[14.]

I had much to think about as we climbed back up the stone stairs to the exit.

For discussie:

- *What did you know about labyrinths before you read this chapter? Where have you seen labyrinths? What do you think about a labyrinth as a pilgrimage?*
- *Are you familiar with some of the films mentioned? If so, what were the dimensional thresholds in these films?*
- *What did you think about the 'almost heretical' thought about Jesus as 'perfect shaman'?*
- *What is the difference between animism, theism and atheism?*

---

14. *In an unplanned 'coincidence', my first revisitation of the Castle Hill labyrinth - with my wife and a group of students - happened to be on Resurrection Sunday, AD2000. I have since become aware of the widespread use of labyrinths in the alternative worship movement globally. See, for example, www.alt.worship.com.*

Mankind was taught to hope by Christianity,
that is, to look to the future
for the realisation of the true meaning of life.
Emil Brunner

5. When?

... did Europe become 'Europe'?

WE EMERGED INTO THE BUDAPEST SUNLIGHT from the labyrinth, and crossed the square to the St Mathias Cathedral. I noticed a great stone raven perched on the roof, placed there by stonemasons centuries before in honour of the king, whose nick-name was 'Mathias the Raven'. Was it just coincidence that the raven was an occult symbol.[15] Was I beginning to see traces of paganism everywhere now?

We passsed through the huge arched doorway and descended more steps into the dimly lit interior. A liturgy of some sort was under way for a handful of communicants, despite the steady buzz of chatter from tourists.

Although this was her first visit there, Danica began to expound knowledgeably to me item after item of pagan symbolism built into this historic place of Christian worship: architectural details, fertility symbols and wall decorations.

'They had to allow these pagan symbols,' said Danica. 'Otherwise the people wouldn't come to church. They believed in them.'

---

15. *'Raven' is the name of a leading British occult magazine.*

How true that was I did not know. But my encounter with this passionate advocate of paganism was certainly opening my eyes to spiritual realities of the post-Christian New Europe, a Europe that could increasingly resemble pre-Christian Old Europe.

As we walked out of the imposing gothic structure, threading our way through the summer visitors, I tried to explain to Danica that there was often a huge gap between the institutional forms of Christianity she was familiar with, and primitive, biblical Christian faith. Much had been done in the name of Christ which in no way reflected the spirit of Christ.

The Crusades, for example. I told her about the Reconciliation Walk, and the apologies some of my colleagues had recently made to Jews, Muslims and Orthodox Christians down the old Crusader trail en route to Jerusalem, for the misguided pattern of violence and injustice committed under the sign of the cross.

Danica turned on me and passionately exclaimed, 'What I want to hear is an apology for the nine million women killed by the Church as witches!'

Pictures flashed through my mind that I had seen a few weeks before by Dutch artist Rien Poortvliet, of women on torture racks being interrogated by seventeenth century church clerics.

She's right again, I conceded. Maybe the number was inflated, even greatly inflate[16], but was this not again a legitimate complaint pagans had against Christianity? Only it was difficult to imagine church leaders having the courage to address this injustice of the past!

'Danica,' I asked later, *'are* you a witch?

She just smiled and said cryptically, 'We all are here in the Balkans.'

Fault lines
Prospects for Europe these two unforgettable and eye-opening days in Budapest had awakened in me were, frankly, unsettling.

---

16 *A monument on the weighhouse in Oudewater, the Netherlands, commemorates the nine million women Danica referred to. However David Burnett, author of The dawning of the pagan moon, believes the figure to be in the tens of thousands, not millions.*

I will always be grateful for the dialogue which we began then and continued via email, and for the challenging perspectives on the Christian faith from a pagan observer.

But I had been confronted with the spectre of a Brave New Europe, of what Europe might look like if biblical values further faded from memory. I began to ponder the possibility of a 'reincarnation' of that brief but violent episode of recent European history, when Hitler combined elements of paganism with modern technology.[17] The association was a little worrying...

After we finally made it to Sarajevo, I continued to process in my mind the host of questions and issues raised by the past few days. The labyrinth had presented one picture of the choices facing Europe.

Now the view from my window in the Turkish quarter offered another. I could look down the river valley along which the city had spread, towards the synagogue, the Catholic Cathedral and the large Orthodox Cathedral, surrounded by a forest of minarets. I was reminded of the fault line running through this city where Catholic, Orthodox, Jewish and Moslem faiths and cultures had converged for centuries.

The assassination of the Austrian archduke on a bridge only a few hundred metres away from my window had led directly to the outbreak of the First World War.

Burned-out silhouettes of the twin UN office towers, the pathetic press building ruins and the tragic shell of the bombarded library stood as silent witnesses to the merciless encirclement of this whole valley by artillery batteries in the surrounding hills, up to four short years before my visit. Deadly fire had rained down on the helpless citizens of Sarajevo before

---

17 *Although some discount the influence of paganism on Hitler, Burnett (see footnote 16) describes how seriously he took the ancient Germanic gods. Burnett quotes Nigel Pennick, who writes about leylines and energy centres. Pennick quotes Hitler's beliefs that special mountains were energy centres which collect cosmic forces from outer space and channel them into the earth through the ley lines. Hitler wanted to control these special sites and thus gain control over Europe.*

NATO belatedly intervened. Chaos had revisited the Balkans along the fault line of these ancient divisions.

But now I was conscious of other fault lines: those between biblical theism, materialism and paganism. The millennial turnover seemed to be witnessing new transitions between these worldviews. What further changes could these lead to in the early years of the twenty-first century?

'The Continent'?

A few days later, I was back in Budapest to board a train for the long, slow ride to Cluj-Napoça in Romania, where I was to teach in a YWAM Bible course. As the old grey-green Soviet-style carriages trundled east across the flat Hungarian plain towards the hills of Transylvania, I had plenty of time to browse through my notes.

I pulled out a paper I had presented the year before, at a consultation in the Crimean resort of Yalta, on the Black Sea.[18] Academics and professionals from across the former Soviet Union had gathered in a former communist sanitorium, just a stone's throw from the Romanov palace where the famous and fateful summit between Stalin, Roosevelt and Churchill had decided the shape of post-war Europe.

My paper was entitled *Hope's Radical Legacy*, sketching the influence of the Gospel on European history. As I began to scroll through the pages on my laptop, I quickly saw new relevance of my own paper for the questions now fresh in my mind.

I had opened with a reference to the late Bishop Lesslie Newbigin, a mission statesman for over forty years in India. Newbigin had spent his last years back in England challenging western church leaders to recognise the direction in which European society was drifting.[19]

Newbigin raised the question, what had made Europe

---

18. *Hope's radical legacy - the transforming influence of the Judaeo-Christian concept of hope on Europe's identity - for full text see www.hfe/resources*

19. *Lesslie Newbigin (1909-1998) missionary in India (1936-74) and bishop of Madras, wrote and spoke on the theme of mission encounter with western culture, and wrote The Gospel in a pluralist society, among other titles.*

'Europe' in the first place? For 'The Continent' was the one continent which was not actually a continent at all! It was simply the western peninsula of the Eurasian land mass.

Our European forefathers had drifted into this peninsular from the east. They spoke languages–Greek, Celtic, Germanic and Balto-Slavic–belonging to the Indo-European family. Their philosophical ideas, myths and legends, gods and goddesses were extensions of the Asian thought-world, particularly that of India.

Yes, Danica was certainly right about the Old Europeans. They were devout pagans and animists, worshipping and appeasing gods and goddesses whose names and identities were often linked with those of ancient Babylon, Egypt and the east.

If this was so, then how did Europe acquire a distinct identity as a separate continent, and as a civilisation?

What, in other words, had made Europe 'Europe'?

As the train rumbled on towards the Romanian border, I read Newbigin's succinct but profound summary of the European story:

> The simple answer is that about 2000 years ago, dedicated messengers came to Europe with a Book that told a Story that brought Hope, and transformed European society.

Hmmm, I mused. Clearly a different interpretation from that of Danica's 'oppressive bronze-age patriarchal sky-god'! The paper was shedding fresh light on several questions raised in our Budapest conversations. So I read on as if reading it for the first time...

> What then was the source of this unique Book, this powerful Story, this transforming Hope? For it did not originate among those barbarians who had swept into the western end of Asia, nor from the Greco-Roman polytheism that dominated the Mediterranean at the start of the Christian era.
>
> No, its origins were indisputably Semitic.
>
> The Hebrews introduced to the contemporary world a revolution in understanding about reality and about God - and thus about humankind, about history and the future, and about the meaning of life.

Monotheism was belief in one God, and that the cosmos ultimately was personal.

This radical revelation that came through Abraham and Moses, and through Judaism to Christianity, inspired a concept of hope unknown outside of cultures influenced by this Judaic-Christian tradition.[20]

For hope was not universally self-evident. In Europe one often took the concept of hope for granted, largely unaware that *'mankind was taught to hope by Christianity'*, as Swiss theologian Emil Brunner had observed, *'that is, to look to the future for the realisation of the true meaning of life'.*[21]

How radical this hope was, and how different the Hebrew concept of God, becames apparent when observing what a mean bunch of gods Israel's neighbours worshipped.

Yahweh however was totally different. He was infinite and transcendent–omnipotent, omnipresent and omniscient. Yet he was personal and immanent–involved in his creation. He was 'compassionate and gracious, slow to anger, abounding in love and faithfulness, maintaining love to thousands, and forgiving wickedness, rebellion and sin.'

The revelation of such a God inspired hope. Revolutionary prospects opened up for the Hebrews' future. The Children of Israel were to become the People of Hope, radically different from the pagan peoples - because they represented the God of Hope who was radically different from the pagan gods. Israel's very *raison d'être* was to channel hope back into a hopeless world!

Biblical hope begins and ends with the revelation of this God. The answers we give to questions of origins, purpose and destiny, and of ethics, norms and values, are shaped by our beliefs about deity. Such root beliefs determine our values and behaviour.

As the unbroken landscape continued to sweep by, I pondered on the truth that European society had been shaped in the past by the answers to these questions - as would be the Europe of the future.

---

20. see David Aikman, Hope, the heart's great quest, ch.2, 'The Revolution of Judaism'
21. Brunner, Faith, Hope and Love p 43

52

What social values and behaviour would result from Danica's core beliefs, as biblical values waned? I wondered. What kind of government? law? family structures? education? sexual relationships? business dealings?

Then I read something that reminded me of Danica's response to my question about her view of Jesus:

> The animist, classical, or eastern view of reality is trans-historical: *Accidental happenings of history cannot prove eternal truths of reason.*
>
> In contrast, the Hebrew revelation of hope is earthed in a Story, in historical events with historical people. The biblical hope which was to spread throughout Europe in the first millennium was essentially a story, the story of humankind's beginnings and estrangement from the Creator; the story of God's dealing with one man Abraham and his offspring Israel with a view to reconciling all the earth's peoples to their Creator. The Bible is a record of happenings in time and space.
>
> This Story unfolds further into the New Testament, which describes God clothing himself in human flesh in the person of the infant Jesus - an historical person at a moment in history.

'Ha!' I almost heard Danica exclaim. Yes, that would indeed be 'foolishness to the animistic Greeks'! Looking at my own faith now through Danica's eyes was helping me to understand the scorn that Paul, for example, must have faced from his audience on Mars Hill.

> The resurrection of this one man in an ancient middle-eastern land offered hope to the peoples of Europe in the first millennium with an *eternal* dimension: physical death was no longer the final reality.[22]
>
> But Christian hope also claimed a here-and-now, *contemporary* dimension. Hope of heaven inspired hope here on earth - hope of liberation from the fear of demons, spirits and capricious gods; hope of relationship with God the Creator Father; hope of reconciliation with one's neighbour, the breaking of the cycle of vengeance between individuals, families, tribes and nations.
>
> Most of the laws of Moses, and the teachings of Jesus, were concerned with life here and now. The implication of the resurrection

was that with the power of death and sin broken, men and women could experience radical changes in their own life styles.

Thus the Judaeo-Christian concept of hope, with both eternal and contemporary dimensions, was prepared for transplanting among Europe's peoples.

When Paul was led as a prisoner along the Via Appia towards the nerve centre of the Empire, few foresaw that his message of hope would overturn Rome within three centuries. Yet into the disorder ensuing from Rome's implosion came legions of Hope-bringers claiming allegiance to the risen Jesus.

They told the same Story from the same Book. They told it to the Greeks and to the Romans, to the Gauls and the Celts, the Scots and the Picts, the Angles and the Saxons.

Across the channel again, they told it to the Frisians and the Franks, the Allemanni and the Suevi, the Germans and the Goths, the Slavs and the Balts, the Rus and eventually to the Vikings.

They confronted the animist beliefs of Europe's barbarians, often through power encounters. In Ireland, Patrick smashed the altars on which Irish Druids had sacrificed children annually to persuade the offended sun god, *Bel*, to lengthen the days again. In Germany, Boniface exposed the impotence of the thunder god, *Thor*, by felling a sacred oak tree.

They set up communities of young and old which became the buildings blocks of the new order of European society, centres for learning, agriculture, commerce, the arts and even government.
By the end of the first millennium, virtually all the European peoples from the Iberian peninsula to the Urals, from Greece to Iceland, had been exposed to some form of this story.

The new hope inspired by this new set of beliefs led directly to values and behaviours which over the centuries have become known as 'European', and are generally taken for granted as being self-evident and 'common sense'. To the degree that they embraced this hope, their collective lifestyle was transformed.

This hope was the singular factor that made Europe 'Europe', robustly self-aware and distinct from its eastern roots.

I paused to reflect on this sweeping statement, and looked out the carriage window at the distant horizon. If this Story, this

Hope, had had such a far-reaching impact on European life and thought, what would happen to Europe when the Story, the Hope, became neglected, forgotten, lost? I wasn't sure if I wanted to go down that road.

No-one pretends that the kingdom of God had fully come in Europe as the second millennium began. The gospel of hope had indeed transformed culture after culture.

But it was also true that pagan beliefs and practices made deep inroads into Christian traditions, including Christmas and easter festivities as we still celebrate them today. [23]

Others view Europe's history as a synthesis between Christianity on the one hand, and paganism influenced by the Greco-Roman civilisation and humanism on the other. Carl Jung described Europe as a Christian cathedral built on pagan foundations.

I chuckled to myself as I read this oft-cited quote from Jung, the Swiss psychologist, for the first time since our recent visit to St Mathias' Cathedral. What an apt illustration indeed!

Danica had described herself as a pagan, Jungian psychotherapist. Both disciple and rival of Sigmund Freud, Jung obviously had been well acquainted with Europe's pagan undercurrent.

I continued reading:

Christianity may well have emerged from the first millennium as the top-layer, with paganism and humanism as the undercurrent. But the second millennium would see powerful resurgences of neo-paganism.

My own reference here to resurgences of paganism struck me now in a new way. I had just met a new face of paganism. Would it be Europe's brave new face tomorrow?

I read on about how the Reformation recovered the place of the individual in God's plan, faith in the consistency of God's laws and hope in God's rulership over the universe, which became the ingredients of the explosion of scientific enquiry into an orderly universe created by an orderly God.

---

23. Wessels, Europe: Was it Ever Really Christian? pp.119, 145, 153-156

But the new open intellectual climate that followed the Reformation spawned seeds of false hope that would undermine the very faith foundations that made them possible in the first place:

> The Renaissance and the subsequent Enlightenment were a revival of Greek and Roman classicism and elements of their occult and pagan worldview. In short, the door opened for *monism* (the belief that everything is one), *pantheism* (everything is God, God is everything), and *deism* (religion and ethics based on reason).
>
> The most dominant and resilient of these '-isms' was *rationalism* (reason is the ultimate arbiter of truth). Rationalism's consort was *materialism*. Only matter mattered. Non-matter didn't matter. So-called objective reason of the human mind, as a disembodied eye surveying the world without being part of it, was to dominate Europe right up until our own day.

Re-reading my own paper felt like walking through the labyrinth anew. It followed the same progression in worldviews from *animism* to *theism* to *materialism* in the course of two millennia - just as we had done on Castle Hill. It explained how Europeans had embraced and rejected in turn the two first basic options; and how that, at the end of the second millennium, dissatisfaction with the third option had become known as 'post-modernity'.

The scene with the lost schoolgirls returned to mind when I came closer to the paper's conclusion. Where could Europeans turn to at the start of the new millennium? What would emerge out of the chaos caused by the 'failure' of all these *-isms?*

The paper returned to Bishop Newbigin to conclude his argument:

> 'There is a growing scepticism about the earlier claims of science to provide us with the guidance we need,' says Newbigin. 'The vastly expanding influence of astrology and of New Age in its many forms is evidence of this. *It is also a reminder that, if Europe loses the Bible, it becomes once again merely a part of Asia.'*

Yes, that was it! That is what felt vaguely familiar about Danica's perspective, back in my hotel room. It echoed Newbigin's warning that when Europe forgets the Story and loses the Hope, it merges back into its eastern roots.[24]

Although Danica had hardly mentioned the phrase 'New Age', this was clearly her world. Of course, I had been aware of the many books, sermons, magazines and workshops warning Christians for a decade or two about New Age and the occult. Some writers had even dared to ask what the Church should learn from the New Age movement.[25] But for me, New Age had been merely a passing fad, something for others to spend their time analysing and writing articles about.

Now I was beginning to see things differently. Danica, and what she represented, was a likely future for Europe. Far from being simply a relic of the past, Danica was the possible face of the future. The New Europe could again become Old Europe, could journey back to the future ... if our memory of the Story, our grasp on the Hope, is lost.

Europe could become re-*'Orientated'*!

Unless...

I scrolled down to the bottom of the paper:

Europe on the brink of the third millennium has become post-Christian, post-communist and postmodern. But as Peter Drucker has said, anything named 'post-' is temporary. What will come next?

Our Age of Chaos has its parallel with the disorder following the collapse of Rome. The messengers who then provided the building blocks of the new order came with a Story, a Book and a Hope. They radically reshaped Europe's identity. They passed on the ancient Hebrew beliefs of an Almighty God, the Creator of heaven and earth, who had himself become human flesh in the person of Jesus Christ.

---

24. *Newbigin had also warned of a new pagan society in his address "Can the West be converted?", January 1987. The idea that secular society was a kind of neutral world, in which we could all freely pursue our self-chosen purposes, was simply a mirage. We now had a pagan society whose public life was ruled by beliefs which were false. This paganism born out of the rejection of Christianity was far tougher and more resistant to the gospel than the pre-Christian paganisms with which foreign missionares have been in contact during the past 200 years. This, he believed, was the most challenging missionary frontier of our time.*

25. *Two very helpful titles are: What is the New Age saying to the Church? Drane; & Jesus and the Gods of the New Age, Clifford&Johnson*

The Story of Jesus Christ gave hope and intelligibility to the whole of human experience. It provided a new starting point for Europe in the First Millennium.

Would it provide a new starting point for Europe in the Third Millennium?

The Romanian students waiting for me at the station in Cluj-Napoça at the end of my long journey, were themselves a sign of hope for a new beginning. Their country had been recently liberated from an atheistic tyrant, and already they were wanting to be trained to take the gospel of hope to other countries. They had good reason to look forward to a hopeful future. ↙

For discussion:

- Carl Jung described Europe as *'a Christian cathedral built on pagan foundations'*. Why?
- Are you aware of specific traditions and habits from pre-Christian origin that remain in Christian circles?
- Discuss the following: *'The answers we give to questions of origins, purpose and destiny, and of ethics, norms and values, are shaped by our beliefs about deity.'*
- Give a short summary of Newbigin's answer to the question, *'what made Europe 'Europe'?'*
- *'Mankind was taught to hope by Christianity,'* wrote Emil Brunner: *'that is, to look to the future for the realisation of the true meaning of life'*. What hope or future-expectation do polytheistic, pantheistic and atheistic beliefs offer?

When all the alternatives have been explored, 'not many men are in the room' – that is, although world views have many variations, there are not many basic world views or basic presuppositions.
Dr Francis Schaeffer

6. Why?

... paganism

OVER TWENTY YEARS AGO, Dr Francis Schaeffer,[26] dressed in his characteristic Swiss knee-length breeches, warned his audience at the Amsterdam Free University, 'If we fail to root western society back into biblical values, the easy days for Christianity are over.' I still feel the sense of foreboding with which those words struck me sitting in that lecture theatre.

In the early nineties, euphoria and optimism still lingered in Europe after the fall of communism when Sir Fred Catherwood described Europe as 'a house swept clean'. This veteran statesman of the British and European political scenes, a former vice-president of the European Parliament, was addressing fellow evangelical leaders on the first occasion of what has since become the annual New Europe Forum.[27] The ominous implication of this biblical phrase was not lost on his listeners.[28] Not only did Europe face the promise of a new future free of

26. Dr Schaeffer was the founder of L'Abri Fellowship in Switzerland, a spiritual retreat centre for inquiring intellectuals. He wrote many books on Christian apologetics. See bibliography.
27. The New Europe Forum is an annual Hope for Europe event seeking biblical directions for social, political and economic issues facing European Christians today.

communism; it also faced the prospect of 'seven other spirits' re-possessing the house. A spiritual vacuum could not be sustained.

Innocent?
Soon after my Budapest experience, I began to notice the name of Harry Potter appearing on the best-seller lists. Weren't these occult-sounding titles? I wondered: *Harry Potter and the Scorcerer's Stone*. Or was I reading pagan overtones into everything now?

Since then the Harry Potter phenomenon has taken the literary world by storm. In what TIME magazine called 'one of the most bizarre and surreal' success stories in the annals of publishing, four children's titles authored by the previously unknown writer, J. K. Rowling, have toppled such well-known authors as Stephen King, Tom Clancey and John Grisham from the top of adult(!) best-seller lists.

Harry's adventures have been translated into many languages, major and minor, including Icelandic, Basque, Serbo-Croatian, Korean and Chinese.

What are we to make of this strange development at the start of the new millennium? Is this further proof that Danica's world is indeed much bigger than I ever imagined?

For those who have not been caught up in this rage, the fictional Harry Potter is orphaned as an infant when his wizard parents are murdered by an evil lord. He is left on a doorstep to be raised by his aunt and uncle in the world of 'Muggles' or non-magical folk, who hold a 'repressive, medieval attitude' toward magic. Yet it is predicted that there "will be books written about Harry - every child in our world will know his name" (a prediction moving uncanningly towards fulfillment in the real universe!)

Harry's break comes when he later is invited to attend the Hogwarts School of Witchcraft and Wizardry, to prepare him to enter into his true spiritual identity and destiny. On his eleventh birthday, Harry is transported on a magical train to a parallel

28. *For further information, and the text of Catherwood's full address, see www.HFE.org/resources.See Luke 11:24-26.*

magic world, much more exciting and captivating than Muggle 'Flatland'. And so our Harry–and each of his young readers–is initiated into an intriguing world of transfiguration, divination, broomstick flying, dungeons, poltergeists and headless ghosts. *Cool!*

Spells are also part of the fascination Harry Potter's magic world holds for his young fans. Browsing through a booklet entitled, *Why kids like Harry Potter,* I read of a young girl who said she too would love to be able to cast spells on all the bullies at school, and that her favourite character was the poltergeist.

So, is this just perfectly innocent childhood imagination? After all, Christian fantasy writers like C. S. Lewis and J. R. R. Tolkien drew on themes of magic, witches and wizards. Isn't the magical train simply the equivalent to Lewis's magic wardrobe, a dimensional threshold? like the phone booth in the Matrix?

Some Christians have argued that the magic in these books was purely mechanical, as opposed to occultic. Harry and his friends cast spells, read crystal balls, and turned themselves into animals - but did not make contact with a supernatural world. Harry was definitely on the side of light fighting the 'dark powers'.

These comments seem to me to underestimate the significant shift in the 'plausibility structures' - what people consider to be plausible or believable - that has coincided with the millennium turnover.

When Tolkien and Lewis used supernatural themes last century, few believed literally in the reality of witches and wizards. They wrote in an 'age of innocence' (or of unbelief) about such things. Readers understood the tales to be fantasies containing spiritual truths.

But through the cheerful normalcy with which Harry experiences the magical realm, is not Rowling communicating to her global audience of young readers something much more? Namely, that witchcraft, magic and wizardry are normal and good. Anyone who does not accept this obviously is still captive in the dysfunctional world of 'Muggles'.

Today's readers are much more likely to accept the literal

reality of the spiritual realities behind crystal balls and spells. They may not believe in demons or spirits, but suspect there is some kind of spiritual energy or force at work.

As for changing into animals, is this itself not supernatural? I happened to see a film on English television recently about a girl who believed she changed into a wolf sometimes at night and attacked people. Afraid of the harm she might do in wolf form, she eventually found a believer in her story, who helped her get permanently released as a wolf on a secret reservation in Scotland. This new expression of an ancient shamanistic phenomenon certainly stretched my 'plausibility structure', but obviously had an audience sufficient to warrant it being broadcast.

While using techniques of magic and mythical creatures, Christian fantasy writers like Lewis and Tolkien develop their imaginary worlds within their own personal commitment to orthodox Christian belief in a sovereign God. Rowling does not share that commitment. Unlike the Christian fantasies, Harry Potter is a post-Christian creation set within an occult cosmology.

My own rather bizarre and surreal experience in Budapest has aroused in me a strong suspicion that Harry Potter's phenomenal popularity among young and old is a significant indicator, not only of the future, but also the present ripeness of many to enter Danica's world.

Books
In the months following this 'cage-rattling' encounter, exposing my unpreparedness to engage with pagan spirituality, I embarked on a reading programme of books new and old.

The Bible itself assumed new currency as I realised in a fresh way how much God's self-revelation unfolded against an animistic, pagan background.
• **Abraham's** initial calling was out of that hotbed of paganism, Babylon.
• **Moses** and **Elijah** confronted pagan gods, and demonstrated very publicly the reality of Jahweh.
• The **Ten Commandments** were a radical departure from contemporary pagan social codes.

• **Israel** was called to display a lifestyle of obedience and service to a holy, loving God, surrounded by nations lorded over by pagan gods and goddesses.
• **Daniel** served faithfully in a pagan kingdom and even discipled the world's most powerful ruler into faith in the one true God.
• **Paul** found communication bridges for the gospel into the pagan, polytheistic world of Asia Minor and Greece.

No, God was not caught off guard by paganism. However new it may be for me or for the western Church, it was nothing new for the God of the Bible, the Lord of history.

Thomas Cahill's *Hinges of History* series reminded me of the role played by two monotheistic minorities, the Jews and the Irish Celts, in shaping Europe's values and worldview, emerging from polytheistic pagan cultures.[29] Celtic monks joyfully transmitted the good news from one pagan people to another, and evangelised much of medieval Europe. What attracted pagan Europeans to their message then? How could it happen again?

For the first time in my life, I began to read the Greek myths. As well as catching glimpses of what it would mean to live life in the belief that gods and goddesses controlled one's fate, I was fascinated to discover some parallels to the story of Jesus.[30]

C. S. Lewis, I had been told, saw in pagan Greek classics communication bridges for the gospel of Jesus Christ. So a natural choice to read was *Till we have faces*, his 'pre-evangelistic' adaptation of the myth of Cupid and Psyche.

I returned with fresh motivation to Anton Wessels' *Europe: was*

---

29. see bibliography: 'The gifts of the Jews'; 'How the Irish saved civilization'.
30. For example, when Sparta and Athens went to battle, both cities sought divine counsel. The Oracle of Delphi declared that the city whose king died in the battle would win. The king of Athens disrobed and dressed as a poor man, went into battle and died. The Spartans later recognised the body as that of the king of Athens, fled in terror, knowing the oracle had foretold their doom. Christ too was the king who disrobed his glory, came as a humble servant, and was killed... Also the story of Prometheus who seized the fire-light from Zeus, and for this was nailed (some say lashed) on the tartarus rocks of Caucasus Mountains, before being delivered by Hercules.

it ever really Christian?, a study not only of how Christianity had influenced the Graeco-Roman, Celtic and Germanic cultures of Europe; but also of how European Christianity had embraced many old pagan practices. David Burnett's *Dawning of the pagan moon*[31] had been sitting on my shelf unread for several years, until my return from Budapest. With whetted interest I read of how this book about modern pagan culture in Britain resulted from his meeting with a white witch on a BBC panel discussion.

Burnett, a lecturer at All Nations Christian College near London, set out to understand and fairly present the beliefs and practices of the pagan community. He submitted his manuscript to some leading pagans for their comment, who said he was the first non-pagan who had really understood them. They asked if they could use his book themselves!

I found Danica's beliefs reflected in many of these pages.

Options

A recent newspaper heading caught my eye: *If this is reality, we're in real trouble*. The writer was reviewing a so-called Reality TV show of the Big Brother variety, in which a handful of selected volunteers live in an isolated environment for a number of weeks, while their every action can be followed by camera for a purient television audience.

The headline said it all: was this really 'reality'?

I had the same question concerning the 'reality' behind Danica's worldview. If this was reality, I could only see a troubled future ahead.

How could we know what was true 'reality'? I remembered that was the question Francis Schaeffer addressed in *He is there and he is not silent.*

I found my dog-eared volume, unopened for many years. I had bought the book in 1973 back in New Zealand, when working among university students as a travelling secretary for Inter-Varsity Fellowship. At university I had struggled to find a framework to integrate my personal Christian faith and

---

31. *see bibliography: 'The dawning of the pagan moon'*

PERSONAL

polytheism
many gods
    Babylon
    Greece
    Rome
    Celts
    Vikings...
	monotheism
	one God
	    Judaeo-Christian
	    Islam

FINITE   **INFINITE**

atheism
no gods or God
    Enlightenment
    Rationalism
	pantheism
	everything is God
	    Eastern

IMPERSONAL

experience with my academic studies. Schaeffer's books had been lifesavers for me.

In this modest volume, Schaeffer answers the basic philosophical questions of life with the biblical revelation of a personal, infinite God.

'The only answer for what exists is that he, the infinite-personal God, really is there,' he states.

I read again Schaeffer's oft-repeated statement that, while there are many possible details, there were only very few answers to any of the great questions of life.

My thoughts drifted back to the labyrinth of Castle Hill. I imagined walking again through the different phases of history in those corridors, representing the basic worldviews that Europeans had adopted and then discarded in turn: animism, theism and materialism.

The options, while with variations, indeed were few:

- *Everything either had an impersonal or a personal beginning.*
- *Ultimate reality was either finite or infinite.*

I began to visualise a matrix based on these two statements, with vertical and horizontal axes intersecting to create four quadrants: the *impersonal-finite;* the *impersonal-infinite;* the *personal-finite;* and the *personal-infinite.*

There you have it, I thought: four basic options. What worldviews did these four quadrants represent? What answers did they each give to life's basic question about meaning? about a moral framework for life?

Firstly, the personal-finite quadrant of *polytheism*: 'a pantheon of gods and goddesses'. This option we are familiar with from the background to the biblical story, as we have mentioned. Babylon, Persia, Greece and Rome all had their deities who controlled the affairs of men and women.

This was Old Europe's worldview, the view of reality shared with variations by the Celts, the Angles and Saxons, the Franks and the Allemani, the Slavs, the Balts, and the Vikings. Some of the days of the week are still named after such gods (Wednesday from *Woden*, Thursday from *Thor*, etc.).

The great dilemma with finite gods, however, is that they are not big enough. Plato, Schaeffer points out, understood the need for absolutes, or nothing has meaning. Without absolutes, no sufficient basis for morals exist. But the gods were finite, and their behaviour reflected human foibles writ large.

The panoply of gods may answer the need for diversity, but cannot meet the need for unity.

Some New Age teaching also belongs in this quadrant. Often however New Agers tend to 'mix-and-match' between the personal-finite and the impersonal-infinite, between polytheism and pantheism. Danica on the one hand talked of personal dieties like Artemis/Diana, and a personal spirit guide, while on the other talked of a pantheistic Mother Goddess, spirit of the universe.

Ultimate reality under polytheism is the spirit world.

The second option, *monotheism*, the view that ultimate reality is found in one personal-infinite Divine Being. The character and person of God is the moral absolute of the universe. The Triune Godhead answers both the need for unity and diversity.

Here we can find answers for the basic questions of meaning, significance and morals. Both men and women are made in God's image, and hence have a personal beginning, and infinite significance.

Ultimate reality under monotheism is a Personality.

The third option moves us into the impersonal-finite option, *materialism*: This is the option of atheism: there is no God or gods. This is the option of rationalism, and of the secular society that had dominated the western world in the twentieth century, as a logical outcome of the Enlightenment.

But talk of meaning, significance and morals when our starting point is impersonal, when humans can be reduced simply to 'slime plus time', becomes meaningless. How do the particulars, individual objects or beings, have any meaning or significance? No answer has ever been given to that.

When materialistic westerners have talked about morals, they have been living off the memory of the Christian past, plucking the fruit of the fruit of the fruit of biblical values, as Schaeffer often expressed it. If we begin with the impersonal, we can only talk about preferences, but not rights and wrongs.

Only matter matters. Non-matter doesn't matter.

Ultimate reality under atheism is physical matter.

The one remaining option is that impersonal-infinite quadrant is that of *pantheism*: 'everything is God'.

The ancient Eastern religions of Hinduism and Buddhism, as well as much New Age teaching, express this worldview. Schaeffer notes that the use of the root 'theism' in 'pantheism' falsely connotes a personal deity. He calls it 'pan-everything-ism'. The starting point is still impersonal, and thus can give no meaning or significance to the diversity of reality. Morals also have no meaning, as everything in 'pan-everything-ism' is finally equal.

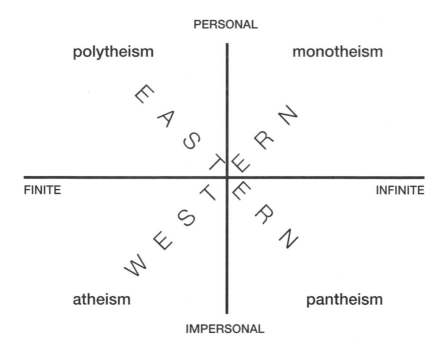

When we start from the impersonal, we arrive quickly at the human dilemma: why should there be any meaning? Humankind is lost. Humankind remains a zero. Personality is reduced to the impersonal.

What ultimately matters under pantheism is feeling and consciousness. Whether through mind-bending drugs, meditation, spiritual ecstacy or sexual experience, objective reality is denied and experience and consciousness elevated.

Ultimate reality under pantheism is consciousness.

The polytheism/pantheism diagonal in the matrix represents the traditional eastern worldviews. We could lump these together, as New Agers themselves seem to do, and call the combined category *animism*, using that word in its broadest sense. We learnt earlier that this was the belief that the physical or natural world was 'animated' by the spiritual or supernatural world.

Correspondingly, we can note that the monotheism / atheism

diagonal reflects predominant western thought over recent centuries. This is the axis where we in the church have felt most at home. Most of the evangelistic efforts and apologetics of the European church have been directed towards the unbelieving materialist, attempting to prove the reality of the spiritual realm and of God.

Yet very little attention has been given to the 'eastern' diagonal in Europe. New pagans, like Danica, are not 'unbelievers'. They believe passionately in the spirit realm. Pagans are not unbelievers in the reality of the spirit world. They are not atheists. 'Signs and wonders' will not necessarily impress them about the spirit world any more than Pharoah's magicians were impressed by Moses - at least, in the initial stages! Somehow they need to be convinced of the truth of that spiritual reality.

This shift of perception of ultimate reality to the 'eastern diagonal' among Europeans will require major changes in the way we conduct our evangelism and engage with pagan spirituality.

Christian psychologist and author, M. Scott Peck, describes Satan as a real spirit of unreality[32] Unless rooted in biblical reality, we *are* in real trouble.

The future of Europe will depend on which view of ultimate reality prevails as the twenty-first century unfolds. Europeans have most recently rejected the materialistic view of reality. That is what post-modernity is all about. Postmodern Europeans are open to spiritual reality.

That leaves a choice between biblical spirituality or non-biblical spirituality, theism and animism. Which will it be?

Could it be that post-modern rejection of Enlightenment values may be leading us back to Pharoah's court and a confrontation between the God of Moses and the pagan gods of new age and new science?

---

32. see Peck, *In Search of Stones*

Ready or not?
We started this section of the book recalling the Y2K scare. The question on everybody's mind then was, are we ready for the new millennium? January 1, 2000 has long since passed. But the question still remains: *Is our enterprise–the church–ready for the new millennium? Are we really ready for the major shifts happening in European and western society? Or will we remain stuck in a time warp, back in the twentieth century.*

In the light of everything we have said thus far, is there hope for our land, and for Europe in the twenty-first century?

I believe there is. And I posit that the following ten imperatives can help us recover faith, vision and hope for Europe tomorrow.

For discussion:

- Why did Schaeffer say: *'If we fail to root western society back into biblical values, the easy days for Christianity are over'?*
- How apt did you find the description of Europe as a *'house swept clean'* at the beginning of the nineties?
- Discuss: *'Some Christians have argued that the magic in these (Harry Potter) books was purely mechanical, as opposed to occultic.'*

Are the choices really limited to these two options:

- *Everything has an impersonal or a personal beginning*
- *Ultimate reality is either finite or infinite;* or do you see other possibilities?
- Make sure everyone understands how the four categories are formed through responses to these two questions. Discuss what the basis is for law, ethics, human values and the family in each category.

Part Two
Ten imperatives

How do we recover faith, hope and vision for the future?

As WE BEGAN *our journey in Part One*
through history's labyrinth together,
we made three declarations:
- *No-one really knows what tomorrow's Europe will look like*
- *Europe tomorrow will not look like Europe today*
- *Most predictions about tomorrow's Europe will also miss the mark*

SOBERED by discovering how limited
our basic world-view options are,
we have caught glimpses of a brave new Europe -
resembling pagan old Europe reincarnated.

STANDING between the times,
we peer into an unknown future.
Are we staring into the abyss?
Or is there a God of hope who is still there,
whose person, plans, promises and power
point to hope and a future for Europe?

WE CONTINUE our journey in Part Two,
in search of grounds for hope...

At the root of history is the One who wills Shalom.
At its end is the One who calls us to Shalom.
Walter Brueggemann

1. Ask!

... what is God's will for Europe

OUR SEARCH TO RECOVER HOPE for Europe begins with this simple question: *what is God's will for Europe? for our country? for our town or city?*

If we have a sneaky suspicion God's patience is exhausted with Europe, that prodigal Europe has squandered all her chances, that God has foreordained Europe to become the end-time Beast, then we will certainly find little ground for hope. Somehow we evangelicals seem to have a hangover from nineteenth-century teaching that things were destined to head downhill towards the end of history.

But if we were to conclude that fatalistic pessimism did not square with the Bible's revelation of God's person, his plans and promises, perhaps we would be prepared to look at Europe's future with a fresh open mind.

At the risk of sounding naive then, let's ask: *Is it God's will for God's will to be done in Europe?*

The answer of course is yes! By definition. God wants his will to be done - here in Europe! Here in our land! Even here in our town!

Then why is there such a lingering Europessimism among

'Bible-believing' Christians? Why do we seem reluctant to believe God's will could–even partially–be realised in Europe?

Ah, but what is God's will? And who can presume to know it?

Hope and healing

Frank Buchman gazed out from high above Lake Geneva in Switzerland on one of the world's most breathtaking vistas. The snow-sprinkled French Alps stretched before him along the blue lake waters towards Mont Blanc. Above him towered the turrets of the eight-storeyed Caux Palace, Switzerland's largest and most prestigious hotel when built in 1902.

But what most inspired the Lutheran evangelist, on this July day in 1946, was his inner vision. He had no doubt what God's will was for a Europe emerging from the chaos and suffering of World War Two. For decades he had preached a message of submission to God's will for individuals and families, and also for kings, presidents and nations. Now, after the turbulent years of global conflict, Buchman was leading a global movement known as Moral Re-Armament (MRA) in the task of remaking the post-war world.

His vision of individuals and nations living in common obedience to God was becoming more of a concrete reality that day with the re-opening of Caux Palace as a Centre for the Reconciliation of the Nations.

Just weeks before, ninety-five Swiss Christian families had given sacrificially–family jewels, life insurance policies, holiday money and even houses–to purchase the run-down asylum for war refugees. Re-named *Mountain House*, the palace was to become a refuge of hope, a place for healing the past and forging the future. Over the coming years, thousands upon thousands of politicians, educators, trade unionists, captains of industry, students, journalists, artists, businessmen and religious leaders from across Europe and the world would come through its doors.

As Buchman entered the cavernous reception hall, he surveyed the colourful gathering where delegates from across Europe, some in national costume, mingled with flag-bearing youths, Swiss donor families and volunteer workers.

Suddenly he asked out loud, *'Where are the Germans?'*

A stunned hush fell over the crowd.

'You will never rebuild Europe without the Germans!' he added, breaking the awkward silence.

Although a year had passed since hostilities had ceased, Buchman's question still shocked many of those present. But he knew if Germany was not embraced by Christian forgiveness and reconciliation, godless forces of anarchy or communism would fill the post-war vacuum. For him, forgiveness and reconciliation were clearly part of God's will for Europe in 1946.

Transformation

'I *hated* Germany so much I wanted to see it erased from the map of Europe!' confessed Irène Laure, a member of the French Resistance at the next summer's conference.

'But I have seen here that my hatred was wrong. I want to ask all the Germans present to forgive me.'

Those Germans present at Caux that summer were among the first of over 3000 leading citizens given special permission by the Allied authorities to travel to Caux to meet their opposite numbers from Europe and other continents. The message of forgiveness and reconciliation taught by Buchman and demonstrated by Irène Laure affected them deeply. They invited Mme Laure to address many of their *Länder* parliaments.

The following year, 450 Germans visited Caux. Among them was Dr Konrad Adenauer, the future German chancellor, who invited MRA teams to bring the message of forgiveness through travelling musical shows, and arranged a series of official receptions for Buchman. In the heavy industry area of the Ruhr many marxist trade union leaders were converted. The resulting moral transformation was seen as a significant factor in the recovery of post-war Germany.

Meanwhile, the French Prime Minister, Robert Schuman, had heard that remarkable changes of heart were taking place in industrial circles in the north, where tensions had led to talk of civil war. The changes were traced to Caux. So in 1948 Schuman arranged to meet the MRA leader.

Buchman's ensuing friendship with both Schuman and Adenauer fostered a change in attitude between the two leaders from mutual suspicion to respectful confidence. This trust culminated in an event now celebrated annually throughout the European Union on May 9, known as Europe Day. For on that date in 1950, the French Government accepted a bold plan, proposed by Schuman and supported by Adenaeur, to integrate the coal and steel industries of France and Germany, and of any other European country who wished to join. Since these industries would be the motor of any potential military machine, future war between the nations would be rendered permanently impossible.

This *Schuman Plan* gave birth to the *European Coal and Steel Community*, ECSC, the first major step toward the formation of the *European Economic Community*, which has grown to become today's *European Union*.

A few weeks later, Schuman decorated Buchman as a Chevalier of the Legion of Honour, in recognition of his role in helping "to create the climate in which the new relationship between France and Germany had been rendered possible."

As we begin our search for grounds of hope, I tell this remarkable story for several reasons. Few Christians today seem to know about the climate of humility, forgiveness and reconciliation which fostered the birth of the ECSC and thus the EU. The Caux story demonstrates the role of a 'faithful minority' in exercising a disproportionate influence on the course of events. It affirms that changed nations begin with changed men and women. It illustrates how God's blessing can spread like an oil fleck into every nook and cranny of society when his people seek to live radically by his principles and character.

This is a story of God's action among the nations of Europe. It gives us hope for his purposes for Europe - even in the twenty-first century. For Buchman in post-war Europe, God's will could be understood from knowing his character and plans. Clearly it embraced forgiveness and reconciliation, restoration and renewal, rebirth and rebuilding.

Today over fifty years later, we will also find the answer to the question, 'What is God's will for Europe?', in his *person*, his *purposes* and his *promises*.

Grounds for hope

Hope begins and ends with the revelation of God. Biblical hope is not mere wishful thinking. It is not a cross-your-fingers or touch-wood superstition. Biblical hope is 'an anchor for the soul, firm and secure', grounded in the revelation of God, his person, his purposes and his promises (Hebrews 6:18,19).

God's self-revelation to Abraham and later to Moses began a radical revolution in understanding reality. He was 'the compassionate and gracious God, slow to anger, abounding in love and faithfulness, maintaining love to thousands, and forgiving wickedness, rebellion and sin' (Exodus 34:6,7). *Wow!* What a God! If that was true, there was indeed hope! The future had revolutionary prospects!

The Children of Israel were to be the People of Hope, radically different from the pagan peoples because they represented the God of Hope, a personal living God radically different from the pagan gods. Even when Israel failed, God's faithful love–his *'hesed'*–for Israel was unconditional, as Hosea the prophet demonstrated.

Despite Europe's unfaithfulness through the centuries, God still pursues her as Hosea pursued his wayward wife. Because of their personal experience of God's *hesed*, Schuman and Adenauer could reach out in hope and trust to one another and create a new beginning for Europe.

The *person* of God is the ground of our hope!

God's revealed *purposes* also embrace all people of all peoples - German and French, Russian and Chechnyan, Serb and Croat, Armenian and Turk. He wants no-one to perish: *'I take no pleasure in the death of the wicked, but rather that they turn from their ways and live'* (Ezekiel 33: 11). God is not only the hope of Israel, he is the hope of all nations. Israel was given the special task of being 'priests of the kingdom' to the world, mediators between God and the nations. They were phase one of his rescue plan activated by humankind's rebellion. The goal was to restore the nations to God's original purpose: unbroken relationship with him, and to be agents of his rule on planet earth. Despite the Eden disaster, there was still hope!

Yet his purposes went even further than that. They embraced the restoration of all things in the cosmos to their God-ordained purpose (Colossians 1:20). Paul describes the whole of creation as waiting in the hope of liberation from sin's fallout (Romans 8:19-25).

The *purposes* of God are the grounds of our hope!

Tightly interwoven with the person and purposes of God are the divine *promises*. History does have a goal. Unlike eastern or animist religions, where life is seen as an endless procession of cycles, God has declared a climax to history. His kingdom, his rule, his reign, his shalom, would eventually be established on planet earth. Just as a river eventually finds its way to the sea, no matter how many twists and turns en route, so too history would eventually climax in the fulfilment of God's purposes. God promised under oath that history would not end until all peoples on earth had been blessed through Abraham's offspring.

While the prophets were often seen as doomsayers, in the long run they were hope-bearers. Isaiah, Jeremiah, Ezekiel and Daniel all promised the ultimate realisation of God's plans. Minor prophets like Hosea, Joel, Habakkuk and Zechariah also promised what God would yet do in history to fulfil his purposes. The central theme of these promises is the coming of God's Reign, the Kingdom of God, his Shalom, on earth.

The *promises* of God are the grounds of our hope!

In the light of God's unchanging person, purposes and promises, we need to throw off those ideas and influences we have collected over time in a hundred subtle ways - ideas that cheat us of faith, hope and vision.

We need to reject the enemy's disinformation!   ↙

For discussion:

- Is it God's will for his will to be done in your town or city? in your country? in Europe? or is this just a naive question?
- Did any in your group know anything about Frank Buchman and Moral Rearmament story? Share what else you knew.
- Had you ever thought that God may have been involved in the formation of the EU? Or did you suspect the EU was just a human initiative – or even diabolical?
- *'Today over fifty years later, we will also find the answer to the question - What is God's will for Europe? - in his person, his purposes and his promises.'* Is this so?
- *'The Children of Israel were to be the People of Hope'* – what did that mean?

When (the devil) lies, he speaks his native language,
for he is a liar and the father of lies.
Jesus

2. Reject!

... the enemy's disinformation

JOSEF GOEBBELS, HEAD OF THE NAZI MINISTRY OF PROPAGANDA, was
one of Hitler's most strategic henchmen. The pen was his
weapon, words his ammunition. He aimed his disinformation at
the perceptions of both the German people and their allies, as
well as their enemies. Clever deployment of truth and distortion
was effective in causing action in the wrong places and inaction
where most needed.

Propaganda is a powerful tool for immobilising opposition by
manipulating truth and perceptions. Some propaganda is crude,
blunt and obvious. Yet victims of the best propaganda are
unconscious of being manipulated.

How do we know we are not being manipulated by our own
governments? The Nazis certainly had no monopoly on
propaganda in the Second World War. Neither did Milosevic
during the more recent Kosovo bombing.[33] Nor Saddam during
the latest Gulf War! The film *Wag the dog!* explored presidential
manipulation of the public via television.

The Bible talks of an adversary who opposes God's plan with

---

33. *see for example Ellul, Propaganda,; and Ignatieff, Virtual War - Kosovo and beyond,*

every trick in the book, fair or foul. Jesus called him the 'father of lies'.[34] How conscious are we of the immobilising effect of his disinformation?

If he can trick us into believing that the future is his, that we Christians are insignificant and have no authority, he has won the battle. His propaganda renders us passive and disengaged. It causes action in the wrong places and inaction where needed.

Three common strategies Satan uses against believers are intimidation, temptation to escapism, and distraction.

Intimidation

Sometimes as I travel around Europe's cities, I experience moments of being overwhelmed by the immense man-made structures of glass and steel, sprawling urban conglomerates, teeming populations, clogged motorways and endless rows of apartment blocks - the immensity and apparent permanency of our civilisation.

Once, as I rode up the escalator of the Metro in Paris, stately buildings came into view, proud and imperial, almost shouting at me, *'Who do you Christians think you are?' 'What do you think you are trying to do?' 'Do you think you really have the corner on truth?' 'Do you think you really have anything to say to our sophisticated society?' 'Why don't you just accept the status quo?'*

I felt simply intimidated.

In moments like these, I have learnt to reflect on Paul's arrival in Rome. How must he have felt as a prisoner of the world's greatest military and imperial power? A skinny, bandy-legged, hook-nosed shipwreck survivor, chained to guards, a figure of humiliation for all who bothered to glance in his direction!

For the first time in his life, he was now entering the hub of civilisation, the greatest and proudest city built to date. Glistening temples, triumphant monuments, shimmering marble edifices, bronze statues and gardens watered by fountains shouted in chorus at him, *'Who do you think you are, Paul?' 'What do you think you are trying to do?' 'Do you think you*

---

34. John 8:44

*really have the corner on truth?' 'Do you think you really have
anything to say to our sophisticated society?' 'Why don't you just
accept the status quo?'*

Perhaps Paul felt the same sense of intimidation. If so, it was
momentary. For Paul knew who he was, and what he was trying
to do. He knew the One who was Truth. His heart burned with
a message about the future for Imperial Rome. For him the status
quo was merely the established disorder of things. His task was
to help overthrow that disorder.

Paul had an inner vision of a different future, the future of
God.

He knew that future to be more real than the temporal, visible
trappings of Roman power and glory.

Rome's glory didn't impress him. God's glory did.

Rome's future didn't impress him. God's future did.

Even under house arrest, Paul declared the present and
coming reign of God.[35]

Jesus Christ, not Julius Caesar, was Lord of history.

Jesus Christ, not Augustus, Tiberius or Nero, was Lord of the
future.

Time passed.

Rome fell.

Paul's message triumphed.

Revelation

In the spring of 1981, in communist Poland, I had a flash
revelation which radicalised my future expectations. I was
invited to speak at a student conference in Warsaw on the
subject: *'An historical and cosmological view of the Church'*.

So, after consulting the dictionary, I headed off east from
Holland with my friend Erik in his yellow Mercedes. Across
West Germany we drove non-stop and arrived at the border
crossing on the Iron Curtain.

Although not my first crossing into the Soviet bloc, the
foreboding sight of the grey kilometres of no-mans-land remains

---

35. Acts 28:31

etched in my memory. A gauntlet of high razor-wire fences rolled down a shallow valley carpeted by acres of grey concrete, snaking around anti-tank barricades towards the grey buildings of the East German check-point. Eagle-eyed soldiers in great-coats and grey watch-towers looked down on our slow-moving Dutch car, machine guns at the ready.

How permanent and impenetrable everything seemed to be! And how grey!

Warsaw however, was anything but grey. Excitement was in the air! These were the heady days of *Solidarity*, the trade union movement emerging from the Lenin Shipyards in Gdansk to challenge the Soviet system. Bright Solidarity posters covered walls all over the city. It was May Day weekend, traditionally the day for national parades displaying socialist glory and triumphs. But for the first time, the marxist government had been forced to bow to an increasingly bold public and not enforce compulsory participation in the parade. Later we heard it had been a pitiful straggling affair.

The students were almost euphoric too. If and when the Russian tanks came, they told us excitedly, they would simply turn all the sign posts around! Erik and I felt apprehensive. Surely they knew about Hungary in 1956? and Czechoslovakia in 1968? The Poles had nothing to stop Russian tanks. And they could not rely on the West's help. We were excited for them, but secretly wondered if future history books would record the next Soviet invasion as Poland, 1981.

Against this background, I stood behind the lectern to talk as requested about the role of the people of God in history and the cosmos. We traced the unfolding story of God's plan and the forming of his people Israel–and later the church–as God's primary change agents of history.

Together we turned to the story of Daniel to catch a glimpse of where history would eventually bring us. In chapter two we read about Nebuchadnezzar's disturbing dream he couldn't remember or understand. God however gave Daniel the dream's description and interpretation: of a statue representing empires present and future, each smashed by a stone uncut by human hand. This stone represented the coming of the Reign of God, and grew into a large mountain filling the whole earth.

By now I was waxing eloquent to the students about all the empires of history which indeed had come and gone: the Babylonian, Persian, Greek and Roman empires, and on and on through the centuries up to the Third Reich. Hitler had boasted it would last a thousand years - yet like all the others, it too had been destroyed!

Suddenly I heard myself blurting out the following unpremeditated statement: *'The Marxist empire too has come, but it also must go! There is only one unshakeable kingdom - God's kingdom!'*

I gasped to myself in shock. What was I saying?! This was a public gathering! There could be informers here! I could be in real trouble. Besides, where had that thought come from? I had never had that thought before! Immediately I realised I had believed 'enemy' propaganda much of my life. I had believed that Marxism was to be here for ever and ever, amen!

Suddenly I saw that we as God's people had had more faith in Marxism's immutability than in the unshakeability of the kingdom of God! We had believed the enemy's disinformation - and it had scared us into paralysis.

That impression of impregnability and immutability I had had crossing through the Iron Curtain; the bombastic rhetoric of a Khruschev thumping his shoe on the UN podium in New York shouting, "We will crush you!" to the world's gathered leaders; all the well-meaning Christian sermons, magazines and paperbacks declaring communism to be the anti-Christ of Revelation that would one day rule the world - these and many other conscious and unconscious impressions over the years had conspired to buttress a faith in the permanency of Marxism.

Now in this instant I realised it was a lie! That's not what God's Word said! Marxism–just like all the kingdoms and empires before it–would also be smashed by the Kingdom of God, the bedrock of reality. Anything that was not based on that kingdom would be shaken and broken. That was true of Marxism. It was true of Islam. It was true of secular humanism.

(Later some students said they had wanted to clap and shout when I had spoken the unspeakable publicly - but the walls still had eyes.)

From that moment, my future expectations changed. As we drove around the city in Erik's car, I dared to wonder if what we were seeing were the cracks in the mighty communist edifice that would spell its downfall. After all, this popular surge of rebellion had been spawned two years earlier when a million Poles had gathered to celebrate mass with their compatriot, John Paul II. People power was in the air, led by Solidarity and personified by a shipyard electrician named Lech Walesa.

Red and white Solidarity stickers were defiantly displayed on the glass doors of the hotel across the road from our lodgings where we went for breakfast. We had heard a rumour that Walesa usually stayed in this hotel when in town. Soon after we sat down, the rumour was confirmed when through the doors burst a small entourage surrounding a familiar stocky figure with a walrus moustache, Walesa himself.

As they settled around the table next to ours, I reflected on my new revelation. What role might this lowly trade unionist be playing in the unfolding purposes of God for Europe and the world?

Yet my apprehension lingered. Would we one day read in the papers about Walesa's sudden disappearance, as we had about other dissidents in Poland? Would he end up incarcerated in a Soviet prison?

I was not yet bold enough to believe we may have been sitting next to the first president of a democratic Poland!

The rest is history. Eight years later the Wall came down.

Recently I drove back from eastern Germany passing through what used to be the Iron Curtain check-point. I had to look hard to recognise the location. Gone were the grey towers, the grey concrete acres, the grey-clad soldiers, the razor-wire, the anti-tank barriers, the impenetrability, the immutability.

Gone! Dumped on history's trash heap.

As predicted by Daniel.

Who do we *really* believe is in control of history?

'To suggest that any other is in charge, to name any other name, other than the Lord of disrupting, abiding freedom, is to answer wrongly. It is to embrace idolatry,'[36] writes Walter Brueggemann.

Wrongly perceiving who is in charge is idolatry.

Do we really believe that the future belongs to the kingdom of God and to the people of God? Do we really believe that one day the kingdoms of this world *will* become the kingdom of our God and of his Christ, and he shall reign forever![37]

Is our hope *really* in the biblical God?

Or have we been seduced by another vision of the future?

Escape

Fatalistic end-time scenarios can blind us from seeing opportunities to shape the future.

Charles Spurgeon warned about this when he thundered from his nineteenth century pulpit in London that *'David was not a believer in the theory that the world will grow worse and worse, and that the dispensation will wind up with general darkness, and idolatry... The modern notion has greatly damped the zeal of the church for missions, and the sooner it is shown to be unscriptural the better for the cause of God.'*[38]

Speculation often results in fear and paralysis. When Christians look towards the rapture as an escape mechanism from the mess on this world, this is exactly what our enemy wants. He knows the followers of Christ are to be God's change agents on planet earth. So his propaganda aims to make us passive and disengaged.

During World War II, my father served with the New Zealand troops in the British Eighth Army in the Middle East. As Hitler besieged Stalingrad in 1942, the Allied command feared the Russians would capitulate and join the Nazis in a coalition of convenience. The threat was so real that troops from the Eighth Army, including my father, were sent to the Syrian-Turkish

36. *Brueggemann, Living Toward a Vision, p.58.*
37. *Rev. 11:15*
38. *Spurgeon's commentary on Ps.86:9, quoted in The Puritan Hope, Murray p.xiv.*

border. They had orders that, in the event of Russian capitulation and a Red Army attack on the oil-rich Middle East through Turkey, the Eighth Army were to fight a delaying action. They could retreat as far as the Valley of Megiddo in Palestine (Israel today). There they were to dig in and fight to the death.

Churning around in my father's mind was the oft-taught scenario of the 'king of the north' (the Russians? Gog and Magog?) converging in Palestine with the 'king of the south' (Field-Marshall Rommel in his seemingly unstoppable charge across the Sahara towards Egypt?)!

He remembered vividly my grandfather's bible prophecy charts which all climaxed at Armageddon, when the nations of the world gathered for the final battle. He recalled the many evangelical books mushrooming in the pre-war years to prove Mussolini's rise to power would revive the Holy Roman Empire, and that the gathering storm clouds would fulfill the visions of Revelation.

The pieces were all coming together to shape a paralysing end-time picture!

'This is it!' he thought. 'I'm going to be in the Battle of Armageddon!'

But my father never fought in that battle. It simply never happened.

He was however in the Battle of El-Alamein, where Rommel was eventually stopped, and the war took a significant turn.

More than half a century after that war, my father could look back over a prolonged period of peace and prosperity, a future he sometimes despaired of ever seeing as a young man. He often told this story to younger generations to warn them not to waste their best years speculating about fatalistic future scenarios, no matter how convincing they may appear.

Rather, he urged them to grasp every present opportunity to help shape the future.

Fatalism about the future has also lead to a shrunken understanding of the gospel, as we shall explore in a later chapter. Some have called this the *Great Reversal*,[39] as it reversed evangelical attitudes towards the gospel's power to transform society at the time of the Evangelical Revival in the eighteenth century. Major social reforms had resulted directly from the revival.

But on both sides of the Atlantic, the later nineteenth century saw a doom-and-gloom eschatology encouraging the faithful to seek the shelter of the church-ghetto, keeping a low social profile while awaiting the Second Coming.

Missiologist Jim Engel writes:

> 'Legendary evangelist Dwight L. Moody correctly captured the mood of evangelicals at the end of the 19th century when he declared, *I look upon the world as a wrecked vessel. God has given me a lifeboat and said to me, 'Moody, save all you can.'* Dreams of transforming society with the gospel had been dashed after the (American) Civil War (since society would be transformed only by Christ when he returned in glory). This left only one option: a single-minded focus on evangelism as the mission of the church.

> 'What a contrast to John Wesley's vision of the church as a body *compacted together ... to overturn the kingdom of Satan, and to set up the kingdom of Christ.* Wesley and others demonstrated in the 18th and 19th centuries that disciples are made through evangelism coupled with sweeping social transformation.' [40]

Concurring with Engel, fellow missiologist David Bosch expected such a pessimistic understanding of history to discourage virtually every attempt at reforming the world and human conditions. 'A fixation on the parousia at the end (the Second Coming) simply means that we are evading our responsibilities in the here and how.' [41]

Popular evangelical apocalypticism continued into the Jesus Revolution of the 1960's and 1970's with books predicting the triumph of the communist anti-christ and stressing the imminence of Christ's return. Best-selling 'Rapture' novels still promote such short-term thinking at the start of the twenty-first

39. see Moberg, *The Great Reversal*
40. '*Getting Beyond the Numbers Game*', James F. Engel, *Christianity Today*, November 2000
41. Bosch, *Transforming Mission* p.505-6

century.

Such influences do little to build faith, hope and vision for tomorrow's Europe.

Distractions

But more dangerous than either of the above tactics for current generations is the adversary's subtle use of *distraction*. He lulls us through comforts and seduces us with temporal pursuits.

No sooner had the year of the Orwellian nightmare–1984–slipped safely by when culture critic Neil Postman pointed out that, while the west may well have escaped George Orwell's dark vision of Big Brother domination, a 'slightly older, slightly less well known, equally chilling' vision predicted by Aldous Huxley in *Brave New World* could well be right on target.

Huxley and Orwell did not prophesy the same thing, said Postman.

Orwell warned of being overcome by an externally imposed oppression. But Huxley saw no Big Brother required to deprive people of their autonomy, maturity and history. Rather, people would come to love their oppression, to adore the technologies that undid their capacities to think.[42]

In *1984*, people were controlled by inflicting pain. In *Brave New World*, they would be controlled by inflicting pleasure.

Orwell feared that what we hate would ruin us. Huxley feared that what we love would ruin us.

'What Huxley teaches is that in the age of advanced technology, spiritual devastation is more likely to come from an enemy with a smiling face than from one whose countenance exudes suspicion and hate,' explained Postman.

Those guarding against tyranny failed to take into account man's almost infinite appetite for *distractions*, Huxley warned.

'In the Huxleyan prophecy, Big Brother does not watch us, by his choice. We watch him, by ours.'

Did you catch that?! We watch Big Brother!

At the century's turn, the very name 'Big Brother' had come to

42. Postman, *Amusing Ourselves to Death*, p.vii

mean so-called 'reality-tv' soaps, where a number of random men and women were confined to sealed-off quarters. All their comings and goings, including showering, defecating and sex, were followed by a mass audience degraded to vulgar voyeurism. The producers seem to be bending over backwards to keep to Huxley's script!

Postman concluded: 'When a population becomes distracted by trivia, when cultural life is redefined as a perpetual round of entertainments, when serious public conversation becomes a form of baby-talk, then a nation finds itself at risk; culture-death is a clear possibility.'

We were, he said, amusing ourselves to death (a-muse: without thought). Our minds and spirits were being dulled.

This is fertile soil for the kind of pervasive social propaganda French Christian philosopher Jacques Ellul warned about two decades before Postman:

'When man will be fully adapted to this technological society, when he will end by obeying with enthusiasm, convinced of the excellence of what he is forced to do, the constraint of the organization will not longer be felt by him; the truth is, it will no longer be a constraint, and the police will have nothing to do.

'The civic and technological good will and the enthusiasm for the right social myths - both created by propaganda - will finally have solved the problem of man.'[43]

Immune?
Surely however Christians are not caught in this trap? Surely believers are more immune to this distraction process than their non-believing neighbours!

Futurist Tom Sine laments, as he surveys the global situation, that much of the Western church is locked into a dualistic worldview that accepts unquestioningly modernity's view of reality and the better future.

In seminars and workshops the world over–including many in Europe–he has been forced to conclude that the vision of the

43. Ellul, p.xviii

future most Christians want comes from modern culture, not the Bible. This renders them vulnerable to the technological distraction of a *Brave New World*.

Sine and others call it *McWorld*, a world in which technology, efficiency, material progress, economic upscaling and consumerism combine to create modernity's vision of the better future.

'Over time, modern Western society has come to define the good life in largely economic and materialistic terms. Most of us, whether evangelicals, mainliners or Catholics, seem to have accepted without question that the better future means getting ahead in our individual careers, in the suburbs, and in upscaling our individual lifestyles. Like our secular counterparts, we seem to have bought into the notion that the more we own, the more we are.'[44]

He agrees with Os Guinness that evangelicals have been forced into the role of cultural imitators and adaptors, rather than originators. In biblical terms, it is to be worldly and conformist, not decisively Christian.[45]

Sine sees this as a crisis of vision. Many of us he says have simultaneously embraced two different images of the better future, neither of which is biblical.

The first image is of a non-material heaven in the clouds. The second is defined primarily in economic, material terms, the McWorld future.

'As a consequence, many Christians wind up with a dualistic view of God. Their God is active in their spiritual lives and shows up at prayer meetings, but is impotent to act in the larger, more natural world until the curtain comes down.'

Such schizophrenia subverts our ability to provide an authentic witness of God's new order, God's better future.

Desertion
When we succomb to any of Satan's strategies of intimidation,

---

44. Tom Sine, *Mustard seed versus McWorld*, p.159
45. quoted in Sine, p.147

temptation to escapism, and distraction, the result is apostacy - that is, we move away from where God posted us–*(apo* - away; *stasis* - stand)–we desert our post.

Yes, we must reject the enemy's propaganda about the future. But our adversary has another very effective tactic: *amnesia.* We also need to remember the truth about the past.

For discussion:

- What is the effect of propaganda? Give examples from recent world news.
- Has anyone in your group seen the film *Wag the dog*? Have them explain the place of propaganda in the film.
- The purpose of propaganda is to create a certain view of reality. Why is this important?
- Do you ever feel simply 'intimidated' by the apparent permanence of the status quo? Discuss the example of Paul in Rome.
- What were the two visions of 'Big Brother' of Orwell and Huxley, and where does *reality-tv* fit in their scenarios?
- What is the 'crisis of vision' Sine sees?

Forgetfulness leads to exile whilst remembrance is the secret of redemption.
Baal Shem Tov
(quoted on the Wall of Remembrance at Yad Vashem, Jerusalem)

3. Remember!

... what God has done in the past

IF MY EXPERIENCE IS ANY GUIDE, books about church history should be packaged with a government health warning: *Danger - may be hazardous to your faith!*

Studying history at university raised major questions for me about the church and Christianity. Terror, oppression, bigotry and violence unleashed in the name of Christ, the Cross and the Church banished me into an agnostic wilderness for about eighteen months of my student life.

Church history seemed to be anything but an inspiring account of faith, hope and love in action.

We have to admit that there's many a skeleton hiding in the church's closet. And we need to respond appropriately. We'll look at that in our next chapter, for there can be no future without forgiveness and reconciliation.

But there's something more dangerous than studying church history. And that's *not* studying church history!

We can be easily robbed of our heritage when we don't know what we are losing. And when we forget what God has done in the past, we forget what he can do again in the future.

Short memories produce short sightedness.

God spoke very clearly to Israel about the dangers of amnesia. In Deuteronomy 8, Moses speaks God's warning to Israel, as they prepare to enter the Promised Land: *Remember! Remember the way I led you, fed you, shod you... Be careful that you do not forget...! Remember the Lord your God! If you ever forget the Lord your God, you will surely be destroyed.*

But, as Moses expected, Israel did forget. And, as God warned, they were robbed of their inheritance again and again, a theme developed in the book of Judges.

To their credit, the Jews did learn–the hard way–to develop a long memory. Their survival has depended on it. Through their faithful reading of the Torah and annual celebration of their feasts, including the Feast of Tabernacles, when they build and live in makeshift shelters to taste life in the wilderness, they remind each other of God's interventions in their history. That has given many of them faith and hope for the future. The Israeli national anthem is not for nothing called the *Hatikvah,* the Hope.

If we want to be people of hope today, we need to remind each other what God has done in the past. We need to develop long memories.

Secret

Earlier we referred to Jeremiah, often seen as a pessimistic, apocalyptic figure calling down doom and destruction on Jerusalem. But wait a minute! Was Jeremiah really a *Jeremiah?* Was he a grumbler and a doomsayer? The more I study Jeremiah, the more I feel he's had a bad press through the centuries. In fact, I have come to see him as a great prophet of hope. He knew the secret of hope.

• *Remember how he bought that field when enemy soldiers were encamped on it? What a declaration of hope for the future! (32:1-44)*

• *Remember the lesson he learnt from the potter who remade the marred vessel? Creative destruction was a necessary part of the restoration process. (18:1-6)*

• *Remember the word of encouragement he sent to the exiles in*

Babylon? God's plans were plans to prosper them and not harm them, plans for hope and a future (29:11)

No, Jeremiah was not a *fatalist*, an *escapist*, a mere *optimist* nor a *pessimist*. He was what I'd call a *biblical realist*. And his responses to the tragedies of his day model for us how to face whatever the future will bring.

Whatever that will be, it could hardly be as severe as the tragedy that engulfed Jeremiah. There he stood in the midst of Ground Zero of his day - the rubble of the temple of Jerusalem, the levelled symbol of God's presence, focus of the nation's hope for generations. God seemed to have deserted His own people, who had now been carted off ignominiously into captivity. The unthinkable had happened. As unthinkable as 11 September.

In Lamentations, Jeremiah vents his feelings: *My groans are many and my heart is faint! (1:22) My eyes fail from weeping; I am in torment within... (2:11)* The hurt is real. He faces the present reality squarely. He describes it as it is.

Then, right in the middle of his dirge, Jeremiah suddenly finds the grace to say: *Yet this I remember, and therefore I have hope. The steadfast love of the Lord never ceases. His mercies never come to an end. They are new every morning. Great is Your faithfulness... (3:21-23)*

This was Jeremiah's secret: *Yet this I remember...!!* He remembered the truth about God, and his hope is restored. He now faces his current realities in the light of a greater reality, the Ultimate Reality. He doesn't deny the terribleness of his current reality. But he receives grace to see it in new, eternal perspective.

Hope comes through remembering the truth about God - his character, his actions in history and his promises for the future.

Identity

My friend Al Akimoff, whose family feld from the Ukraine in the days of Stalin, told me the following story.

When Stalin took over the Ukraine, he invited all the blind musicians–*khabzors*, as they were known–to a special gathering. In cold blood they were all mown down and buried. But why? How could these poor blind people be a threat to a mighty tyrant like Stalin? The wily dictator knew that these people held the key to the identity to their land – their memory.

For, robbed on their faculty of sight since birth, the *khabzors* had the best-developed memories. From their childhood they had been trained to set the history of their land in music form. They travelled from town to town, and from city to city, singing their songs at feasts and other important gatherings. The *khabzors* were the memory of the people. They maintained the identity of the land, with their historical perspectives, and helped the Ukrainians remember who they were.

Stalin knew that the old memories had to be erased in order to teach them his vision of a marxist, utopian future. He wanted to rewrite history and shape the future. He could only build his new communist society on such a foundation.

How effectively has our memory been erased? What do we still know of our rich heritage of a faithful minority which has had disproportionate influence on the course of history?

Bias

Every history book is written from a certain perspective and with particular faith assumptions. Postmodernists have reminded us that no historical account is truly objective. Just as every photograph is taken from a certain angle, so every historical account has a bias. That's true no matter how detailed the treatment might be - whether Gibbon's ten-volume *Rise and Fall of the Roman Empire,* Churchill's umpteen volume *History of the English-Speaking Peoples,* or Latourette's seven-volume *History of the Expansion of Christianity.*

Loren Cunningham, YWAM's founder, tells audiences to imagine watching their favourite football team on television. You soon find yourself growing discouraged, he explains, as you realise the cameras focus only on the opponents scoring goals against your team. What the cameras do not show however is that for every goal scored against them, your team has scored two!

That's how the media often handles the good news of what God is doing in our world today, says Loren. That's also how history books have often handled the good news of what God has done through a creative, faithful minority throughout the centuries.

Church history so often focuses on emperors and popes, kings and princes, bishops and priests–the rich and the powerful–who let the side down again and again. History is usually recorded by the conquerors, the powerful, the elites, spin-doctored to make themselves look good.

We have to learn to read history differently.

How then does God view history?

Luke gives us a clue in a passage reeking of irony - chapter three, verses one and two:

> In the fifteenth year of the reign of Tiberius Caesar–when Pontius Pilate was governor of Judea, Herod tetrarch of Galilee, his brother Philip tetrarch of Iturea and Traconitis, and Lysanias tetrarch of Abilene–during the high priesthood of Annas and Caiaphas, the word of God came to John son of Zechariah in the desert.

In the desert!! While all the big-wigs were in their palaces, robed in their royal raiment, the King of the Universe chose a nobody in the desert, dressed in animal skins, to herald his Kingdom!

Translated into our contemporary political situation, at the time of writing, this passage could read as follows:

> In the fourth year of the presidency of George W. Bush–when Tony Blair resided at Number 10 Downing Street, Gerard Schroeder ruled over the Reichstag and Jacques Chirac presided over the French Republic–while John Paul II was still pope in the Vatican, the word of the Lord came to John Everyman in the countryside.

Throughout history God has called faithful nobodies to herald his Kingdom - the weak and the poor to confound the strong and the rich. Sine calls this God's Mustard Seed conspiracy.

Some see history shaped by impersonal, irresistable forces - laws of dialectical materialism, historical determinism or plain fate. In this view of history, you and I are insignificant.

Others talk of History Makers, the great names we learn about at school: Alexander the Great, Julius Caesar, Cleopatra,

Charlemagne, Napoleon, Lincoln, Hitler, Churchill, Gorbachev, and so on. Again, since you and I don't get our names in the headlines, we appear to be of little significance to history.

The Bible however gives remarkably little attention to the big shots. If they are mentioned, its usually in the side margins. That's not where the real action is, from God's perspective.

His main interest is with a faithful few, often anonymous to the world, men and women who live by their inner vision of a better future, God's future; hope-bringers, trouble-makers, dissenters, people who refuse to accept the status quo, who have turned the world right-side up, and who have made a disproportionate impact on the human story.

You and I are invited to join this faithful few, to live towards a vision of a different future, to join the Mustard Seed conspiracy, to be part of the yeast of history doing its quiet, hidden, essential work - and to discover our true significance in history.

Surprises

What will we discover if we begin to read history in search of this company of the faithful? We will discover the God of surprises! the God of his promises! the God of new beginnings! the vanishing God who reappears in unexpected places! And we will grow in our anticipation of more surprises in the twenty-first century.

We will learn about the anonymous thousands of early believers who simply 'gossiped the gospel', as J. B. Phillips put it, and added to the church daily in their normal social intercourse as traders, merchants, tutors and soldiers; and who grew in number until Rome was forced to eradicate or embrace this faith.

We will witness a dramatic turning point in 312 when Constantine adopted a form of Christian faith as he became emperor, ending decades of ruthless persecution; and yet making the church chaplain to the state, redefining 'church' and 'believer', which in turn resulted in widespread nominalism and lax spiritual standards and creating a legacy of institutionalism still with us today.

We will see a dynamic, new movement of spirituality bursting out of the Egyptian desert(!) to inspire many similar movements up through Palestine and Syria, Turkey, across to Gaul and eventually to the far-flung corner of Europe, Ireland. This movement–*monasticism*–transforms the pagan Celts within a generation, and continues to sweep back through Scotland and England, and across to the continent, like a wave rebounding off a seawall. Celtic messengers bring hope and faith to Scots and Picts, Angles and Saxons, Franks and Friesians, Bavarians and Allemanni, and, eventually, the Vikings, transforming many of Europe's pagan tribes. Historian Thomas Cahill attributes the Celts as having saved western civilisation. (This Celtic movement demands closer investigation in the light of today's challenge of a neo-paganism.)

We will watch new reform movements emerge in response to corruption and unbiblical practices in the church early in the second millennium, including the Great Schism with the Eastern Church, the misguided Crusades, and the Inquisition; movements like the Franciscans and Dominicans which remained within the Roman Church; and others like the followers of Waldo, Wycliffe and Hus, who were forced out of the Church, setting the stage for Europe's second great divide.

Social conscience

We will observe the Reformation erupting across Europe in the 1500's, recovering the key Biblical truth of salvation by faith, and releasing a spirit of enquiry into the Book of God's Works, Creation, thus giving birth to modern science; as well as provoking the Radical Reformation which restored biblical definitions for 'church' and 'believer', insights which eventually found their way back into mainstream Protestantism leading to the Evangelical Revival in the eighteenth century.

We will encounter dynamic social change in what John Wesley called 'godless' England, triggered by an aroused social con-science, including the ending of slavery, the protection of women and children in factories and mines, the ten-hour working day, prison and hospital reform, the emancipation of women, the nursing profession and hospitals, orphanages, education for all, trade unions and more. Other nations followed suit, creating many of the social institutions taken for granted in modern democracies.

We will note how the modern missionary movement follows this revival, as men and women like William Carey and David Livingstone dare to believe that God wanted to transform society after society around the world through the message of Jesus. Such pioneers were not just interested in 'saving souls' or planting churches. They were also pioneers in agriculture, forestry, education, science, astronomy, commerce, printing, publishing, banking, development work, healthcare, social justice and setting up libraries. Their understanding of the Great Commission involved much more than just Bible translation and the making of converts. It embraced teaching a whole people and society how to live to serve God the Creator. As with Wesley in England, their passion was to see the reform of the whole land and Christ's lordship extended over all of life and society.

We also see how other European countries, entering the Industrial Revolution, were significantly influenced by biblical visions of reality. The key figure in the transformation of Norway from national poverty to wealth in the beginning of the nineteenth century was Hans Nielsen Hauge. Hauge and his followers led a renewal movements within the church, which had nation-wide influence on agriculture, education, publishing, politics and trade.

If Wesley can be called the apostle of England, and Carey the father of modern missions, Hauge can surely be called the father of modern Norway.

In the nineteenth century a Christian entrepreneur by the name of Raiffeissen brought hope to thousands of German farming families, when he set up networks of cooperatives banks, guided by biblical social principles. The name is still a leading entity in banking in German-speaking Europe and in Holland as the *Rabobank* (*Raiffeissen-Boerenleenbank*).

One of the fathers of modern Holland is unquestionably the remarkable figure of Abraham Kuyper – journalist, theologian, educationalist, politician and prime minister. His impact on Dutch life at the end of the nineteenth century and the beginning of the twentieth has left an indelible imprint on churches, schools, the media and politics for more than a century.

What was the secret of this exceptionally productive man, described by one of his opponents as having ten heads and a hundred arms?

On the occasion of the twenty-fifth jubilee as editor of *de Standaard*, Kuyper said:

> One desire has been the ruling passion of my life. One high motive has acted like a spur upon my mind and soul. It is this: That is spite of all worldly opposition, *God's holy ordinances shall be established again in the home, in the school and in the State* for the good of the people: to chisel as it were into the conscience of the nation the ordinances of the Lord, to which Bible and Creation bear witness, until the nation again pays homage to God.

Such a survey of history will help us realise that God is indeed the God of new beginnings - and that again and again in depressed periods of history, God the Holy Spirit has turned the page and begun a new chapter.

In short, by recovering our memory, we will recover hope ... for our own countries, and for Europe! Yes, we do have a rich heritage! And that we must not forget. But this is not the whole story. If we are honest, the glory of our heritage is also tarnished by much shame. How should we respond to this?

For discussion:

- Read as a group Deuteronomy 8. How relevant is this chapter for God's people today?
- How much of the historical perspective presented in this book is new to you?
- What did author Tom Sine mean with the expression 'Mustardseed conspiracy'? What can this means now in our society?
- How did mission pioneers like Carey and Livingstone interpret the commission to 'make disciples'?
- A century ago, Kuyper wanted *'God's holy ordinances to be established again in the home, the school and in the State'*. How relevant is that in our present multicultural society?

The Church cannot cross the threshold of the new millennium
without encouraging her children to purify themselves,
through repentance, of past errors and instances of infidelity,
inconsistency and slowness to act.
Vatican Document on the occasion of the Jubilee year, 2000[46]

4. Admit!

... honestly the sins of the church

EARLY IN 1993, I STOOD WITH MY COLLEAGUE, Lynn Green, on the north side of Old Jerusalem's massive grey-white stone walls, east of the Damascus Gate. Together we read a bronze plaque announcing that at this spot, on July 15 1099, Godfrey de Bouillon had breached the walls of Jerusalem and had taken the city for the Crusaders.

At high school I belonged to a Christian club called *Crusaders*. I wore a lapel badge depicting a white shield with the red St George's Cross, embellished with a sword and a helmet. A Jewish classmate would ask me in disgust why I wore that badge. Didn't I know, he would ask me, that the Crusaders raped and pillaged their way across Europe towards the Holy Land? Frankly, I didn't. Crusaders were heroes, weren't they? And Billy Graham held 'Crusades' too, didn't he?

Lynn now filled in the details not mentioned by the plaque. After breaking through these walls, he explained, the Crusaders had herded Jews into a synagogue, setting them alight in one

46. *Memory and reconciliation: the Church and the faults of the past, December 1999*

great holocaust oven. Terrified Moslems had fled into a mosque on which the Crusaders had raised their banner indicating a safe haven, only to be slaughtered by the soldiers of Christ wading knee-deep into the defenseless crowd. After three years of killing Eastern Orthodox Christians, Muslims and Jews in similar holocausts on their expeditions down through Europe and into the Middle East, the *militia Christi* then knelt and gave thanks to God for delivering the city into their hands.

As the 900th anniversary of the First Crusade approached last decade, Lynn believed it was time to re-evaluate these events. It was high time Christians humbly and sincerely apologised for these misguided and destructive expeditions of sanctioned 'Christian' violence in which the cross was inverted into a sword, hacking out a blood-stained legacy across Europe, the Middle East, history and current events.

The devastating events of the Crusades–there were eight in total–have remained bitter memories between East and West. They have continued to influence social, religious and political relations not only in Europe and the Middle East, but also in today's global politics: including the Gulf War, Russia's fears of NATO's eastward creeping borders, and even the latest terrorist attack on New York's World Trade Centre and the Pentagon.

Epiphany
On July 15 1999, exactly nine hundred years after Jerusalem's 'liberation', and after three years of retracing the First Crusade route down through Europe towards the Holy City, Lynn and a group of over four hundred Christians representing thirty-three different nations gathered in Jerusalem for a solemn assembly. They looked back over those past three years, starting at Cologne Cathedral at Easter 1996 - years in which Jews, Moslems and Orthodox Christians had opened doors of hospitality in country after country to over two and a hlaf thousand westerners delivering a simple apology, acknowledging the wrongs of the crusades:

> Nine hundred years ago, our forefathers carried the name of Jesus
> Christ in battle across down through the Balkans and into the Middle

East. Fuelled by fear, greed and hatred, they betrayed the name of Christ by conducting themselves in a manner contrary to His wishes and character. The Crusaders lifted the banner of the Cross above these people. By this act they corrupted its true meaning of reconciliation, forgiveness and selfless love. On the anniversary of the first Crusade we also carry the name of Christ. We wish to retrace the footsteps of the Crusaders in apology for their deeds and in demonstration of the true meaning of the Cross. Their path went through your land. Their actions left their mark on your people. We deeply regret the atrocities committed in the name of Christ by our predecessors. We are simple followers of Jesus Christ who have found forgiveness from sin and life in Him. We renounce greed, hatred and fear, and condemn all violence done in the name of Jesus Christ. Where they were motivated by hatred and prejudice, we offer love and brotherhood. Jesus the Messiah came to give life. Forgive us for allowing His name to be associated with death. Please accept again the true meaning of the Messiah's words:

The Spirit of the Lord is upon me, because he has anointed me to bring good news to the poor. He has sent me to proclaim release to the captives and recovery of sight to the blind, to let the oppressed go free, to proclaim the year of the Lord's favor.

As we go we bless you in the name of the Lord Jesus Christ.

A Moslem cleric in Cologne, at the start of the Reconciliation Walk, had said whoever had conceived this plan must have had an epiphany. Religious and governmental leaders everywhere had welcomed the initiative with warm gratitude.

In Turkey, television and newspapers had given the walkers priority coverage. Mayors of cities in the Levant and the Middle East had hosted banquets to honour the walkers. The Mayor of Tel Aviv had told them, 'Peace will come to this part of the world through people like you.'

Yet what had meant most to the team members was the reception they had received along the route, being waved into houses and being offered tea, coffee or cold drinks. Many well-wishers lined the roads offering encouraging words, often expressed in tears. The depth of the wounding caused by this shameful phase of Christian history was evident in the outpouring of gratitude expressed towards the walkers.

Now finally in Jerusalem, the group split into three delegations. The first brought an apology to the Greek Orthodox Patriarch, Diodoros, who responded,

'We are thankful to all of you who undertook another kind of crusader walk, coming to ask forgiveness for those who suffered and endured difficult trials for many years. May our Lord forgive all of us. We are inspired by our Lord to forgive and forget. We thank you for coming, even though it is late.'

A second delegation went to the Great Synagogue, where the Chief Rabbi of Western Jews, Rabbi Lau, replied:

'Today is 15 July 1999. The Crusades were the cause of much bloodshed in the Islamic world and the Jewish world. To meet here after 900 years means that we have learned something from history. The cynics say that the only thing that we learn from history is that we have learned nothing. Your visit shows the contrary. We want these events never again to occur.... There is no reason for bloodshed. This evil century in which we are living started with those events 900 years ago. We hope this is the end of it.'

The rabbi was all too aware that Hitler had justified the Holocaust by what had been done to Jews in the name of the Church.

The third delegation was welcomed in East Jerusalem by Sheikh Sabri, the Mufti of Jerusalem and Palestine. After listening to Lynn's message of apology, Sheikh Sabri revealed centuries of pent up frustration towards Europe:

'We welcome this delegation of Christians to apologize for the Crusades. Some of you are descendents of the Crusaders and some of us are descendents of Saladin Ayubbi, the famous Muslim leader who liberated us from the Crusaders. We are still suffering from the politics of the governments of Europe; it hasn't changed since the Crusades. We have our hope, and we ask your delegation to use your influence on your governments to change their politics. We hope that we arrive at a time when all are treated equally. We wish you success in your mission to bring your message.'

Skeletons

Without forgiveness, there is no hope and no future. Healing begins when we honestly face the past. Desmond Tutu dramatically underscored this truth over the last decade as he nurtured his nation from black-and-white polarity towards rainbow diversity, chairing the South African Commission for Truth and Reconciliation.

As with Nehemiah, we need to admit and confess the wrongdoings of our spiritual fathers (Nehemiah 1:6). Church history has many shameful pages. Skeletons galore lurk in many a church cupboard. Sins of commission and omission have contributed to today's spiritual landscape in Europe. Yesterday's wrong choices and actions have granted spiritual powers legal rights and footholds in countless situations across the continent. They have spawned grievances and resentments between people groups and religious communities, generations and genders, social classes and nation states. Wounds have remained unhealed. Guilt has remained unresolved.

Today's headlines from Bosnia, Kosovo, Chechnya, Russia, the Middle East and Northern Ireland have roots centuries-deep. Very often, arguments among God's people have been the initial cause. It is no coincidence that the Crusades were initiated less than fifty years after the Great Schism between the Eastern and Western Churches, leaving a spiritual, political and cultural faultline scarring Europe today. And the occasion of that Schism? A hair-splitting argument over whether the Holy Spirit proceeded from the Father *and* the Son, or from the Father *through* the Son! Orthodox theologians accused Rome of blasphemy by demoting the Holy Spirit to the lowest level of the Trinity.

Unresolved legacy

What then can we, God's people, do about past wrongs? Isn't this a task for the EU? or the UN? or NATO? Is there really any point in getting involved in issues that have become so politicised? Perhaps not, if the root of an issue was simply political or military. But if such conflicts were the legacy of sectarian strife within the Body of Christ, or, as in the Crusaders' case, misrepresentation of Christ's message, then only Christ's followers could really do something about the root problem.

No other group or institution can apply the atonement of Jesus Christ to situations of conflict. This means confessing the truth about unjust actions of our tradition or people, turning from unloving to loving responses, extending and receiving forgiveness with old enemies, and doing what we can to restore damage and injustice.

Paul John Paul II has been very conscious of this truth and has worked courageously on numerous fronts to ask forgiveness on behalf of the Roman Catholic Church. In May 1999, he became the first pope in history to celebrate the eucharist with an Orthodox leader, the metropolitan of Romania, in a conscious effort to restore fellowship broken by the Schism.

The Crusader spirit carried over into the voyages and exploits of the Conquistadors, the Inquisition which continued into the nineteenth century, Europe's role in the slave-trade and even into Europe's colonialism. Walking down the Greenwich Meridian Line through England and France into North Africa has been YWAMer David Pott's way of encouraging an appropriate response to the still unresolved legacy of slavery's shameful chapter in history.

The list of past sins and mistakes demanding present responses from the body of Christ is depressingly long.

Personal
All of this may seem very distant from daily life at the office. But as we read the paper on the train to work, or watch the evening television news, we cannot escape being reminded of the consequences of lack of forgiveness, however far away in time or distance. This is true at all levels of society - in our families, neighbourhoods, cities, nations, and internationally. For missions is all about the reconciliation of individuals and families with God's original purposes, of communities and neighbourhoods with God's will, of cities, peoples and nations with God's intentions for them.

The principle of confession and forgiveness lies at the heart of the Christian message and lifestyle. Every time we say the Lord's Prayer we are reminded that to receive forgiveness from our Father requires us extending forgiveness to others.

Forgiveness simply makes good sense, as was underscored in a recent article in the Dutch *Elsevier*[47] magazine:

'Apologising is very difficult, if not humbling. Still, it is usually worth the effort simply to say sorry. Verbalising your apology is an exceptionally effective way of burying the hatchet.'

The article lists the rewards of saying sorry as: less guilt, shame and fear, more self-respect, strengthened relationships and prevention of repetition.

If this is true at a personal level–between husband and wife, worker and employer, or teacher and student–how true it is also within a community, or a city, or a nation, or at international levels. Forgiveness is closely linked with our theme of hope and the future.

Without forgiveness there is no hope and no future. Healing only comes when we dare to look honestly at the past. Desmond Tutu has powerfully underscored this truth in recent years when as the chairman of the South African Commission for Truth and Reconciliation he guided his land from black-white polarity towards rainbow-diversity.

Integrity
Recognition of our sins and mistakes is crucial for two other reasons. One, broken relationships rob us as 'people of hope' of our integrity. We simply will not be credible in the eyes of others. We have no message of reconciliation. We do not live the answers. We do not communicate hope by our lifestyle. And secondly, we have no legal authority over our spiritual enemy. We are, in fact, siding with the great disrupter himself, instead of taking our stand with the One who will reconcile all things to himself. Our message is a message of reconciliation, of *shalom*, which is a state of right-relatedness, where everything is relating

and functioning as originally designed.

John Dawson, the current president of YWAM International has joined with others on prayer journeys, diplomatic initiatives and convocations of church leaders to address the deeply-rooted anti-Semitism ratified at the Council of Nicea in 325AD, under Constantine, who concluded: *'Let us then have nothing in common with the most hostile rabble of the Jews...; let us withdraw ourselves from that most odious fellowship.'*

Dawson has initiated the *International Reconciliation Coalition* to encourage believers worldwide in the ministry of reconciliation. He suggests we identify the ancient and modern wounds of injustice, pride and prejudice in our nations needing healing in a biblical way. These could involve conflicts of race, class, culture, gender, vocation, labour and management, regions, religion, nationalities, generations and families.

Dr Michael Schluter is another who has recognised the centrality of right relationships for a hopeful future, and is working hard to make it happen. He established the *Relationships Foundation* in England, based on the ethical values of the Judaeo-Christian tradition, believing that relationships are key to the wellbeing of individuals, families, communities and society as a whole. The relationships are affected by decisions and actions at all levels, from personal to public policy, and that much needed to be done to strengthen relationships across public and private life. This foundation aims then to promote an agenda for social change, by promoting improved relationships through research, practical initiatives and consultancy for organisations and government departments. The Australian Labour Party has established a shadow ministry of community relationships as a result of the influence of the *Relationships Foundation*.

Such issues are not simply to be left to governments and social welfare departments, to professionals and law enforcement agencies. This is a task for people of hope, for those entrusted with a ministry of reconciliation by the God of Hope.

Healing Europe's wounds requires an honest admission of yesterday's sins and mistakes - just as the recovery of faith and vision for tomorrow requires us to face up to the truth about the present. ↙

For discussion:

- What image of the Crusades did you have growing up?
- Read Nehemiah 1:6, 9:2 and Ezra 9:6. Nehemiah and Ezra were upright people, but still they identified with the sins of their people. Why? (See 1 Cor 10:13, Rom.3:23; 7:21)
- Discuss current examples of the consequences of the lack of forgiveness.
- *'Without forgiveness there is no hope and no future.'* Why not?
- Discuss the quote from the Vatican at the start of this chapter.
- Do any of your relatives have something against the church? What can we do about that?
- Where is forgiveness needed in our community? In the light of Ezekiel 22:30, take time to pray about this.

I am French. I am Catholic.
I believe in reincarnation. I am a Christian.
I am an atheist. I am a scientist,
I go to a spiritist healer when I am sick.
I am a rationalist.
Frenchman quoted by David Bjork

5. Face up!

... to the truth about the present

THE HEADLINE IN THE DUTCH CHRISTIAN PAPER READ: *'Europe is still the most Christian continent'*. Quoting the newest edition of the World Christian Encyclopaedia, the paper reported that 537 million Europeans were Christians, more than in Latin America (483 million) and Africa (344 million) or Asia (314 million).

Five hundred and thirty-seven million!! Almost ten times the population of Britain. Wasn't that wonderful? I thought. This was the best news I had heard since the fall of the Wall. All our concerns about Europe had been falsely based! We had been fooled by all those empty church pews. What we thought was a mass exodus from traditional churches both east and west must have been people rushing off to the mission field! We had been misled by stories of a postmodern generation of disillusioned, cynical, non-churched European youth, despairing of meaning and purpose in life.

Reports of growing urban ghettos of migrant children with no Christian roots in our European cities must have been a mis-understanding. All those former communists in eastern Europe had apparently made their way back to the fold of the Orthodox Church, and had stopped dreaming of the 'good, old days' under Marxism. We could be comforted that trends towards legalised euthanasia, same-sex marriage and abortion–led by Christian Holland(!)–were offset by the knowledge that, well, after all, 'Europe was still the most Christian continent'.

All this time we had been grovelling in self-pity, thinking we were just a small faithful minority, like Elijah, unaware of the seven thousand faithful in the land. Hallelujah! But ... where were they all? I began to wonder. I had visited almost all European countries and had not discovered large actively Christian populations.

Or ... could it be that the definitions being used were so broad and all-encompassing–counting anyone who had ever seen a church building or could draw a cross–that such figures were totally useless? I suspected that these definitions included the Orthodox Serbs and Catholic Croatians tried in recent times in the UN Court at The Hague for multiple rape, genocide and other war-crimes. I had seen a lot of crosses drawn on walls in Bosnia staking out Serbian territory. And woe the Bosniac Moslem or Catholic Croat who strayed across the line!

No, I was not yet ready to rejoice over this 'good news'.

Honest

Rather, I was reminded of a much-trumpeted world map showing the current state of world evangelisation which appeared a couple of years ago. It was advertised as the 'most historic and strategic map' ever produced. So I had ordered ten of them. When they arrived, I eagerly pulled the maps out of the carton mailing tube, unrolled them and zoomed in on Europe. What did I discover? More good news! Belgium was already evangelised! and half of France! Wales too, but not England or Holland...

Now, I happen to believe in the motivating power of information. William Carey presented statistics about the world's unreached millions to launch the modern missionary movement. I have been involved in collating research in Holland for the DAWN church planting movement.

But let's get real! I thought to myself. These sort of statistics about Europe meant nothing and helped no-one. It was time for us to get honest about our desperate situation in Europe. Of all continents, ours was most guilty of suppressing the truth about God and exchanging that truth for a lie (see Romans 1:18, 25). That heading would have been more accurate with the alteration of one letter: *'Europe is still the **post**-Christian continent'*.

Now, that term 'post-Christian' upsets some people. Some say it is a negative confession, fatalistically accepting the status quo as irreversible. I do not believe this current state of affairs is God's will for Europe. It should be clear from what we have covered so far that the whole purpose of this book is to help recover faith, hope and vision for tomorrow's Europe. But honest diagnosis precedes effective remedy. It is time to stop pretending.

Dwarves

Compared to the other continents, Europe is fast becoming a continent of spiritual dwarves. Believers in China outnumber the whole population of Germany. There are more Anglicans in Nigeria than in England and America combined. One church in Korea has a membership equal to the whole population of Amsterdam. The Assemblies of God denomination in Brazil has more members than evangelicals in the whole of Europe.

Some years ago, the front page of the International Herald Tribune read: *France is being possessed by the occult*. Now, the IHT is hardly a Christian publication, let alone charismatic or pentecostal. So I read with great interest what a secular journalist would have to say about the country where, during the French Revolution, 'Reason' was enthroned on the altar in Notre Dame Cathedral. France, I read, now had more spiritist healers than doctors, lawyers and priests combined in the whole country, according to records of income tax returns. The Catholic Church itself recognises this reality, has declared France a nation of baptised pagans, and has called for its re-evangelisation.

Ironically, the same country that enthroned Reason on the altar in Notre Dame Cathedal during the French Revolution was now in the grip of superstition and spiritism. While official

Catholic Church figures count forty-eight million Catholics, allowing for drop-outs and minority church streams, others estimate 40.6 million French, or seventy percent of the population, to be Christian.

But how do the French themselves use this word *Christian?* David Bjork, a missionary in France for some twenty years, writes that most French people he knows would comfortably say all of the following: *'I am French. I am Catholic. I believe in reincarnation. I am a Christian. I am an atheist. I am a scientist, I go to a spiritist healer when I am sick. I am a rationalist.*[48]

So when a French person says they are Christian, Bjork explains, it usually has nothing to do with faith. It has everything to do with their culture belonging to Christendom. Bjork questions that Christian France ever existed. Instead, he believes we should talk about 'post-Christendom' France.

France seventy percent Christian??! Fifteen per cent of the French population take anti-depressives, the highest rate in the world, and three to four times as high as the European average. Almost one in three French people live alone. The French crime rate has overtaken that of the USA, and France is the most corrupt industrialised nation after Italy. The divorce rate is forty-one percent and almost half the children are born to unmarried mothers. There are five million alcoholics, and two million regularly use drugs.[49] Marseilles on the Mediterranean coast, one of France's largest cities, has a major moslem presence, with its large migrant population from North Africa.

Christian France? What does that really mean?

Most challenging
We have seen earlier why Bishop Newbigin described Europe as: 'a pagan society whose public life is ruled by beliefs which are false. And because it is not a pre-Christian paganism, but a paganism born out of the rejection of Christianity, it is far tougher and more resistant to the gospel than the pre-Christian pagan-

---

48. see Cahill, How the Irish saved civilization,
49. Memory and Reconciliation; the Church and the faults of the Past, December 1999

isms with which foreign missionaries have been in contact during the past two hundred years. Here, without possibility of question is *the most challenging missionary frontier of our time'*.

Indeed we need to face up to the truth about the present. We are hearing more and more about the apparent demise of Christianity in Europe – and the rise of a new paganism. We have already seen how the two phenomena are linked.

Daily evidence of a rising climate of paganism varies from the sophisticated to the bizarre. Recently my wife and I came across a *School for Earthcare and Spiritual Horsemanship* in the Dutch countryside. A current car model is called *LIANA*: Life In A New Age. A revival of Halloween, formerly foreign to most European countries is being encouraged by commercial interests, capitalising on old pagan Celtic festivities around the New Year (Samhain) feast on October 31. More and more firms and organisations engage in meditation and eastern mystic exercises. Bookstores that used to have a 'religious' section now stock 'spirituality' books, of which the Christian section is often a small minority. Airline magazines tell us about 'soul yuppies', the breed of young, beautiful professionals into yoga, buddhism, pranayama, reiki, astrology, kaballa, mantras, channelling, ashtanga, zen. *It's all cool.*

But what is the basic worldview behind all these hip activities? Basically it is animism. Animists believe the whole world is animate–alive–with divinity, explains Scott Peck: 'Although it can give rise to enslaving superstition, animism may not be that far from the mark. Certainly it expresses a vision of the world that frequently seems more interesting than our own mechanistic and materialistic vision in this Age of Reason.'

And interesting it seems to be for increasing numbers of supposedly sophisticated Europeans today.

Cut-flower
At a *Hope for Europe* women's conference some years ago, each participant was asked to present something to represent their own nation. When my wife walked to the podium with a

beautiful bouquet of tulips, no one needed to ask from which country she came. Romkje went on to explain that while the flowers were beautiful at that moment, everyone knew what that same bouquet would look like in two weeks time. Each of those tulips had been cut off from its roots, and was doomed to wither. That was the sad reality about Holland, she explained, unless somehow Dutch society could be rooted book to the values out of which it originally grew. A hush of recognition fell on the audience. These tulips–while indeed universally identified with Holland–could represent almost any European nation today.

The raw truth is, we are living in a *cut-flower* society. Certain values and institutions have grown out of biblical revelation and out of past revivals, helping to make western society humane. Concepts we take for granted like human rights, liberty, education for all, the dignity of the individual, the sanctity of life, grew out of a soil impregnated by biblical truth, a biblical understanding of humankind.

Europe today is living on the memory of such Christian values. As Dr Schaeffer expressed it, Europeans are enjoying the fruit of the fruit of the fruit of biblical truth, without being conscious of the origins. You don't need to be a rocket scientist to predict what eventually happens to flowers when they have been cut off from their roots.

When communism imploded, politicians thought that mere transplantation of democracy and free market principles would be the solution for the former Soviet Union. But democracy and free market principles came out of the soil enriched by biblical truth. Without that kind of spiritually-enriched soil, such 'flowers' cannot bloom.

Aleksandr Solzhenitsyn's advice to his fellow Russians on rebuilding society's foundations apply equally to the west when he says:

> The strength or weakness of a society depends more on the level of its spiritual life than on its level of industrialisation. Neither a market economy nor even general abundance constitutes the crowning achievement of human life. The purity of social relations is a more

fundamental value than the level of abundance. If a nation's spiritual energies have been exhausted, it will not be saved from collapse by the most perfect government structure or by any industrial development; a tree with a rotten core cannot stand.[50]

What about Islam?

The role of Islam in shaping Europe's future is the subject of hot debate in many circles. Some are convinced that Islam will grow in dominance – if only through biological growth. In some of our cities, the majority of youth no longer have any 'Christian' background. In cities like Amsterdam and Rotterdam, Brussels and Hamburg, the number of non-indigenous youth is fast outgrowing the Caucasian, traditionally 'Christian' youth. The majority of our urban populations will soon be without any exposure to Christianity, nominal or otherwise, in the past.

Well-known English speaker David Pawson, is convinced God has told him England will become a Moslem nation. He hopes he is wrong. I certainly do too. But Pawson is doing us a favour in making us aware that the future will not just be more of the same. What will our cities look like say in ten or twenty years' time with a majority of citizens who have never had any Christian background?

However, since September 11 there is heightened awareness of the issue at all levels of society. The threat of a dominant Islam does not come from its attraction as a religion to indigenous Europeans. Despite a limited number of marriages between Moslem men and European women (rarely the other way around), few Europeans are converting to Islam out of religious conviction.

The far greater ideological conversion that is well under way is to what we have called the new animism, new paganism, in attractive, sensual packaging geared to a generation seeking experience without accountability or demanding morals.

---

50. *Aleksandr Solzhenitsyn, Rebuilding Russia, p.56*

Twilight?

All of this may tempt us to discouragement and despair about the future. But God has not been caught unawares. As mentioned earlier, animism is the background of the Bible. God even allowed an apostate Judah to go into exile to the hotbed of paganism, Babylon, and when the exiles returned to Jerusalem, they were a fiercely monotheistic people, chastened and purified.

What the twenty-first century demands therefore an expression of Christianity that is able to demonstrate the spiritual reality of a God who is there, who does speak and who dwells among his people still today. The Celtic missionaries effectively demonstrated this in earlier times and won our pagan forebears over to faith in Jesus. We must learn again from their example.

We hear much about the twilight of Christendom, and many wonder how much longer the church can survive. Indeed, we are experiencing a twilight, but is it of the Christian faith, or of an institution we call Christendom? This is not the first time in history that observers have predicted the twilight of the Christian faith. And it may not be the last! The eighteenth century French rationalist Voltaire announced Christianity's demise and declared that a hundred years hence the Bible would only be found in used-bookstores. Within fifty years, his own house had become the headquarters of the Geneva Bible Society. Shortly after the American Revolution, fears (and hopes) were expressed that Christianity would not survive into the next generation. Then came stirrings in prayer, and prayer concerts sprang up across the colonies, eventually fanning into flame the Great Awakening that has left a profound imprint on American society.

Sometimes we have the idea that the course of Christianity in history has been a parabolic path like that of a cannon ball, and that we are now experiencing the inevitable demise of the church. But, more realistically, the course of faith through the ages has resembled trading on a busy day at the stock market, with many ups and downs!

Dusk or...?

Yes, we do see a twilight – but is it not the twilight of modernity? And with that, the twilight of Christianity in its 'modern' expression? The Spirit of God, as we have said before, is the God of surprises. And he breaks out with new life from the most unexpected corners, at the most unexpected times, in the most unexpected ways, to confound all the predictions of the experts!

As on Good Friday, when to the disciples all seemed to have been lost and all hopes crushed, God's hidden grace is still at work, and Sunday is coming!

Far in the Arctic north, the summer sun nevers sets. In late afternoon, the fiery ball sinks towards the horizon. But before it disappears, its trajectory levels out around 'midnight' and begins to climb again. For a few minutes, dusk and dawn seem to merge.

This millennium change may yet prove to be such a 'midnight' moment. Will historians later look back to recognise the dawning of a new day in the dramatic story of the Jesus movement.

Yes, it's high time to be honest about present realities. It's also time to recognise the signs that God is up to something new...

↙

For discussion:

- *'Honest diagnosis precedes effective remedy.'* What would an honest diagnosis of our town/city reveal?
- Why did Newbigin describe Europe's new paganism as *'undoubtedly the most challenging mission frontier of our time'*?
- Give examples of non-biblical spirituality in your area.
- What is the influence of Islam in your neighbourhood? How does that compare with ten years ago?

See I am doing a new thing!
Now it springs up; do you not perceive it?
I am making a way in the desert,
and streams in the wasteland.
Isaiah 43:19

6. Look!

... what God is up to

NOTHING IS PERMANENT. The break-up of the hated Berlin Wall and the awful collapse of the World Trade Centre in New York should remind us of this for the rest of our lives.

As we face up to present seemingly permanent realities, such images remind us that all created things will be shaken. Marxism, Islam, western materialism ... all will be shaken. Only that which is unshakeable, God's kingdom, will remain (Hebrews 12: 27).

Let's take a closer look at seven signs of hope that God is up to something new in Europe.

1. The shakings of God
The decade of the nineties was ushered in by dramatic shakings in the Marxist world. Answers to prayers we hardly dared to believe for came in an avalanche of change. The Gulf War was seen by many observers a part of a series of shakings in the Moslem world. Even the terrifying WTC attack reminded us that western materialism was not immune to shakings. I do not mean to imply that God was the ultimate cause of the terrible events of September 11, but he does use crooked sticks to hit straight.

Our world is being shaken in new ways, and we are being reminded that despite the appearance of things, nothing is permanent. Only that which is based on the kingdom of God will survive the shakings, Jesus warned.

Jesus talked of upheavals and shakings as birth pangs of the new order.[51] Even in the midst of tragedy and horror, we can detect the God of Hope at work doing the unexpected. Despite the grim realities we looked at in our last chapter, God is still the God of Hope, and still specialises in doing the unexpected.

2. New spiritual hunger

God is turning up in Europe again - in some surprising places, proclaimed the European edition of TIME magazine in June 2003. 'It may sound strange to say, but in some ways Europe's faith has survived the church,' continued TIME. 'While the continent may be more secular than ever, God hasn't gone away for everyone... In all but a handful of countries, more than two-thirds of people believe in God.'

What then are some of these surprising places where God is turning up? TIME suggests God has *'gone private'*. The separation of church and state, proposed by Anabaptists in the sixteenth century and enshrined in the American Constitution in the eighteenth, is being seriously considered in those last bastions of establishmentarianism such as England and Norway. Citizens, like states, are rethinking their relationships with clergy and fashioning their own relationships with God - from France to Russia. A French theologian is quoted as predicting that 'at the end of this path will open a new age of Christianity.' Truth is, suggests TIME, it may already have begun. Galina, a Moscow translator, confesses that when she goes to her Orthodox church, she avoids making eye contact with the clergy - whom most Russians mistrust: 'the important thing for me is to have God in my heart.'

Traditional services, with the 'hard pews and the drone of the sermons', are described in the report with adjectives like

---

51. *Matthew 24:8*

'bureaucratic', 'obsolete' and 'irrelevant'. Interactive celebrations and studies, where questions are welcomed, are burgeoning across the Nordic region, and via the Alpha course have spread to thirty-eight countries in Europe. Alpha's founder, Nicky Gumbel explains: 'Our society has changed. We don't need to change the message but we need to change the way we put it across.' Reports of YWAM's Impact World Tour events, with break-dancing, skateboarding, trick-cycling, fire-dancing and power displays could have illustrated this category further.

An unexpected rejuvenation of Christianity was under way among European youth, claimed the article. 'An increase in religion among youth is very clear,' stated a French sociologist. Significant increases among youthful believers were cited in Denmark, Italy and even France. The village of Taizé in Burgundy continued to attract 100,000 primarily young people each year on an ecumenical pilgrimage. A Swedish bishop was shocked to find himself accompanied by 500 youth on a recent five-day pilgrimage. In Berlin, youth comprised forty percent of the 200,000 gathering for an Ecumenical Church Day in spring 2003 - prompting theologian Hans Küng to assert: 'This is not the end of Christianity at all. When 7000 attended (a workshop) just to hear me answer the question, *Why be a Christian today?* you cannot be a pessimist. I have hope.'

Even in The Netherlands, notorious for its soft-drugs, abortion, euthanasia and same-sex marriage policies, 32,000 young people flocked to Arnhem's Gelredome sports complex the same week as the TIME article appeared, for the annual Evangelical Broadcasting's Youth Day, backing up traffic through the city and creating motorway jams!

TIME also noted what the trend we identified in the earlier chapter: 'God' had gone alternative. People were defining their own belief systems and mixing in alternative spirituality. While many may be rediscovering spirituality, they are not necessarily returning to the church or sticking to its tenets, continued the report. In a postmodern age of mix-and-match, this renewed interest in spirituality can get fuzzy around the edges, borrowing from Buddhism, Hinduism and other sources in a form of 'a la carte' Christianity. The concern of many church leaders was expressed in the report by Godfried Cardinal Danneels, the Archbishop of Brussels and Mechelen: 'The church needs to get to know modern culture. But it's a mistake to think we should try to attract more people by diluting our message.'

So after a century in which Marxist materialism in Eastern Europe attempted to brutalise belief in God out of existence, and in the west consumer materialism claimed to have rendered the Creator irrelevant, spirituality is in again. As John Drane puts it, the overt search for spiritual meaning has never been more intense than it is now.[52] Whether expressed through the unpredictable revival of Gregorian chant music (the cd *'Canto Gregoriano'* made by monks in a small monastery in northern Spain sold over four million copies), or through the spiritual quest of scientists exploring the boundaries of quantum mechanics, popular spirituality is flowering like shoots springing up through cracks in a dry wilderness impoverished by two centuries of secularisation.

Postmodern dissatisfaction with the failure of material progress and scientific achievement to answer the deepest questions about the meaning of life, and post-communist frustration with the bankruptcy of atheistic socialism, have created a generation of Europeans wide open to spiritual exploration - of all sorts.

All too often the Christian God is seen as captive of the traditional church. Yet like Vincent van Gogh, the Dutch artist who rejected the church but remained fascinated with Jesus all through his turbulent life right up to his tragic suicide, young Europeans are not anti-Jesus. They just don't recognise him dressed in his Sunday-best.

We must view this spiritual hunger itself as a sign of hope - and learn new approaches to evangelism not geared to atheistic secularism, but to post-Christian spirituality.

---

52. See John Drane, *'The McDonaldization of the church'*, p.55

3. Stirrings in prayer

The nineties saw many fresh expressions of prayer among Christian believers emerging, including prayer concerts, prayer trip-lets, prayer walking, prayer marches, forty-day prayer and fasting seasons, 24-7 prayer chains and prayer for the Moslem world during Ramadan.

March for Jesus began in London City and spread throughout Britain, across into Europe and then throughout the world, eventually climaxing on June 25, 1994, in the biggest prayer meeting in history involving many millions simultaneously.

During the nineties, thousands enthusiastically responded to calls to *pray and fast*, including many young Europeans who fasted for up to forty days.

Prayer triplets, based on the promise that whenever two or three believers pray in the his will, the Father will answer, brought believers across Europe together in threes, each bringing three other names to pray for.

Reviving the concept of *prayer concerts* that emerged in the eighteenth century during the Great Awakening in America, believers from different churches and streams in one location gathered for concerted prayer for each other, for their town or city, for their country and for the world.

As the twenty-first century began, young people took the lead in initiating twenty-four hour prayer chains for seven days a week in the so-called *24-7 prayer network*, spreading contagiously across national and denominational borders.

Prayer for the Muslim world grew to unprecedented levels globally as the nineties progressed, and millions of Christians joined in prayer during the *Ramadan prayer season* for revelations of Isa (Jesus) to Muslims around the world.

Such new and diverse prayer initiatives involving greater numbers than ever before surely must be seen as a prelude of things to come.

4. New vision for church planting and new forms of church

United prayer has brought leaders to ask the question: how can we concretely pray for our nation? and for Europe as a whole?

What do we mean by the re-evangelisation of the European nations? More mass campaigns? More street evangelism? More evangelism via the media?

Part of the answer surfaced early in the nineties with new vision for church planting. The DAWN vision (Discipling A Whole Nation) caught on in a number of European nations as leaders realised that, until we plant a fellowship of believers, a witnessing fellowship, into every neighbourhood in every European country, we have not given every European a chance to see and hear the gospel.

The first time I remember someone conducting a spot survey asking a group of believers how many had come to faith primarily through mass evangelism, a mere sprinkling of hands responded. Through street evangelism? radio or television evangelism? literature evangelism? church visitation? door to door evangelism? Still only a few scattered hands were raised each time.

When it was asked how many had became believers primarily through the influence of a friend or relative, a whole forest of hands suddenly shot up!

What does that mean? Of course, we need evangelists like Billy Graham, Luis Palau and Ulrich Parzany, and mass evangelistic initiatives like Impact World Tour. And we need street evangelists, effective literature evangelism and creative evangelism through television and radio. Yet I'm convinced that the vast majority of people are reached through ordinary, faithful believers going about their daily lives!

This means communities of believers need to be established in every neighbourhood to give everyone the chance to rub shoulders with and to interact with believers. In other words, there is no substitute for saturation church planting as an evangelistic strategy.

From that moment on, I saw the task of the re-evangelisation of Europe in a whole new way. In every nation we needed to see a church planting movement, denominations working together towards the goal of saturation church planting. The 'rule of thumb' suggested by the DAWN movement is one fellowship for every thousand people....in every European nation. That would mean 16,000 fellowships for the Netherlands, more than double the present total of congregations, protestant and catholic, liberal and evangelical. Possibly ten thousand new fellowships would be needed in Holland alone!!

In the nineties, the vision for church planting took root among denominational leaders in many European countries - truly a sign of hope that God was up to something new. In England, the DAWn vision influenced every protestant denomination. Ambitious goals were set for 20,000 new fellowships to be planted by the year 2000. At mid-decade, however, new questions began to be asked. Even if these goals were reached, would England be effectively reached? or would the new churches simply be clones of existing churches, reflecting sub-cultures people had already walked away from? What sort of churches would effectively reach England's unchurched?

As the new century approached, church attendance in mainstream Christendom across western Europe continued to wane. Some smaller denominations, particularly pentecostal, bravely showed signs of growth. Others were bold enough to ask out loud, what actually is the church? and how should it look in the twenty-first century? how relevant are forms that developed in the pre-modern or modern eras for today?

Younger leaders began experimenting with non-traditional expressions of church. An awareness of networks of youth congregations developing across the continent led to the *E-merge* gathering of several thousand young Europeans in Frankfurt in the summer of 2001.

The Alpha phenomenon surfaced in England early in the nineties, jumped across the channel to the continent, taking root in most unexpected, conservative circles. Alpha groups introduced the New Testament concept of *koinonia*-based meeting, often in homes and around meals. Many who came to faith through Alpha courses were now hungry for fellowship-based church models, and did not easily make the transition to the existing churches. Seminars introducing cell churches and house churches were attended eagerly by many dissastisfied with old models.

Voices arguing passionately for a revitalisation of worship explored internet links and multi-media possibilities to create an 'alternative worship' movement merging the radical with the traditional, the old with the contemporary.

Yet others dreamed of a church beyond the congregation, a community framework for a lifestyle lived out seven days a week, twenty-four hours a day, a way of living rather than an event attended one day a week.

A godly dissatisfaction seemed to be driving the search for something new, something related to the postmodern world, that sought to transform culture rather than to withdraw from it. This honest quest for a church for the twenty-first century is also a sign of hope.

More about this in chapter nine.

5. Look who's coming to Europe

Yet another indication that God is up to something new is that he is bringing to Europe people from Asia, Africa and Latin America with gifts we have lost: gifts of faith for church planting; gifts of boldness in proclamation; gifts of discernment of the spirit of animism, with which they are so familiar. I suspect God is sending us these messengers to wake us up out of our Enlightment-induced stupor. Like the proverbial frog who gets cooked alive in water slowly heated up, we Europeans are being gradually accommodated to the daily barrage of post-Christian 'non-values'. Brothers and sisters coming from the two-thirds world can all too clearly see that Europe is in 'hot water'.

Ugandan pastor John Mulinde, for example, is a man with a prophetic message for Europe. He promoted a prayer movement in Uganda which has helped turn that calamity-stricken nation around to become the first nation where AIDS is now on the decrease. As Mulinde travels through Europe, he releases gifts of faith among Europeans that prayer really changes things. He tells of Ugandan congregations who are fasting and praying for revival here in Europe!

I recently spent three days in a conference with Africans called to work in Europe as missionaries. They call themselves GATE -

Gospel from Africa to Europe.

In Perm, Russia, I attended a large healing campaign where one of the speakers was a Nigerian, pastor of one of the largest churches in Kiev, the Ukraine - several thousand strong. Some of the largest churches in Amsterdam are also pastored by Ghanaians and Nigerians - in the Bijlmer district, where, because the city planners designed no church buildings at all, believers gather in the parking garages.

If we Europeans don't have the faith for our own continent's future, these two-third worlders certainly seem to. Argentinians and Brazilians have been arriving in groups to pray for Europe in recent years. Latin Americans have become popular conference speakers teaching from their experience of city-wide revivals, and have specifically blessed us in YWAM. I met a Guatemalan heading up a theological seminary in Moscow. Brazilian YWAMers (JUCUMeros) can be found in several European locations from Moscow to Portugal, especially in pioneering situations like Albania and Kosovo.

The TIME report also confirmed that God was turning up among the immigrants of Europe. Under the heading 'Saving the Prodigal Parent', missionaries from the developing world are reported to be 'doing their best to shore up the foundations of European Christianity'. From nations like South Korea, Brazil and Uganda where Christianity is thriving, immigrants to Europe are often shocked by the lack of passion among Europe's Christians. At the same time, these immigrant missionaries see their work as a gesture of thanks to Europeans for bringing the gospel to their countries in past times. 'Before they came, we were worshipping trees and demons,' said an Ugandan pastor now working in Birmingham, England. More missionaries are on the way from these and other countries, and TIME suggests that European immigration officials may have to create a new visa category, distinct from that of asylum seekers: *soul seekers!*

Surely it is a sign of hope that God is laying Europe on the hearts of Koreans, Africans and Latin Americans for prayer - and action.

6. Ecumenism of the heart

A further sign of encouragement is the growth of a climate of unity and cooperation. An ecumenism of the heart–if not of total doctrinal agreement–has emerged over the past decade in many European countries, often promoted by a generation of leaders who worked shoulder to shoulder in interdenominational youth organisations with colleagues from other denominations.

In England, for example, Spring Harvest came out of the Youth for Christ stable to lay a significant foundation for relationship development and teaching across traditional barriers. Of course, the charismatic movement also brought a recognition that the Holy Spirit was no respecter of denominationalism.

Even in Holland (where it used to be said: 'one Dutchman, a theologian; two Dutchmen, a congregation; three Dutchmen, a split...') the nineties saw partnership developing on many fronts, particularly fostered by the Evangelical Alliance, Agape (Campus Crusade), YWAM, the Evangelical Broadcasting Company (EO) and others.

The March for Jesus promoted unity powerfully by encouraging churches everywhere to do something very simple that almost everybody could do: walk together and pray together.

Once more, the Alpha courses are one of the most effective agents promoting this ecumenism of the heart. In towns and cities across Europe, believers meeting together around a meal in private homes or restaurants or halls build relational matrices that cross denominational borders and promote a solidarity among God's people in that locality.

In our own neighbourhood in Holland, Romkje held the first Alpha groups in our living room, after we visited Holy Trinity Brompton in London. Less than half a dozen groups were active in the whole nation. Now Alpha groups have since spread to almost every church in our town, and seven hundred nationally. The result is an unprecedented *ecumenism of the heart*.

In Austria, traditionally a conservative bulwark of Catholicism where evangelicals were barely tolerated as 'sects', a roundtable has emerged in which Pentecostal, Evangelical, Lutheran, and Reformed leaders regularly convene in a spirit of respect and unity not only with each other but also with top Catholic leaders in the country, in honest dialogue and in a recognition that the ground of their unity is Jesus Christ alone.

In the spring of 2004, a new initiative emerged as an expression of this ecumenism of the heart. The debate about the role of God in the new constitution of the European Union brought believers together from different traditions, Catholic, protestant and even Orthodox, to celebrate our common Christian heritage. Under the banner of *Together for Europe*, ten thousand believers converged on Stuttgart, to be linked by satellite to a hundred other European centres, in perhaps one of the largest expressions of an ecumenism of the heart ever.

When Christian leaders come together in recognition of their need for each other, it is a sign of hope. In a later chapter we'll examine this further and share vision on what could happen in Europe if this ecumenism of the heart continued to spread.

But for now, let's recognise God at work.

7. *Reconciliation*

A glimpse back over the past decade could lead us to conclude that this may have been one of the most significant decades in history in terms of reconciliation. Initiatives taken from the Vatican, to start with, not only involve rapproachement with the Orthodox churches over a one thousand year family feud, as already mentioned, but also a significant accord with the Lutheran Church in which Rome recognised that on most scores, Luther was in the right. The pope also apologised for the burning of John Hus at the stake in 1415, an issue of national sensitivity still in the Czech Republic today. This pope was brave enough to do something no other pope in history has ever done –apologise for the sins of the Church–not just for the sins of the sons of the Church! One does not have to be in agreement with all the pope stands for to laud his amazing achievements towards reconciliation.

Countless other initiatives at various levels of officialdom, some more overtly Christian than others, include the Reconciliation Walk along the Crusader trail, reconciliation in South Africa, settlements between the government and the Maori people in New Zealand, reconciliation initiatives between former colonial powers and former colonies, initiatives relating to the slave trade, to the brutal treatment of convicts sent to Australia by British authorities... and on the list goes.

Intention
The shakings of God, new spiritual hunger, new creative prayer initiatives, new vision for fellowships, new waves of Africans, Asians and South Americans bringing new hope to Europe, new ecumenism of the heart, and impulses of the Spirit towards reconciliation – surely these are signs of the divine intention for a new dawn, a hopeful future!

There is yet another significant hopeful sign – growing awareness that the good news involves more than merely securing one's ticket to heaven, important as that may be. For all too often, our understanding of the Christian message could be summed up in the title of the popular film: *'Honey, I shrunk the kids!'*

For, honey, we shrunk the gospel!

For discussion:

- Do you recognise these 'seven signs of hope' from your own experience? If so, give your own examples.
- How does your church or congregation view church planting? Has that perspective changed over the past ten years?
- Has the Alpha course brought change to your neighbourhood?
- Do you have any personal experience with African, Asian or Latin American believers? Which gifts do they bring to Europe?
- Is there a growing 'ecumenism of the heart' where you live? If so, why? If not, why not?

There is not one square inch of the whole territory of our human lives over which Jesus, who is sovereign over all, does not say, Mine!
Abraham Kuyper

7. Recover!

... the gospel of the Kingdom

RIDDLE: THE GOSPEL IS ABOUT JESUS DYING FOR OUR SINS and rising from the dead, thus conquering death and offering us eternal life. Right?

Then how is it possible that, three years before going to the cross, Jesus went about preaching the 'gospel'?

Matthew records Jesus going throughout Galilee preaching the *gospel* of the kingdom (chapter 4:23). Mark writes in his opening chapter that Jesus went into Galilee proclaiming the *good news* of God (verse 14). Luke quotes Jesus at the start of his work saying, 'I must preach the *good news* of the kingdom of God... (chapter 4:43).

What then is this good news? this gospel?

The word 'gospel' itself is derived from the old English *godspel,* meaning good news. So here is Jesus spreading good news about something long before he died and rose from the grave!

The truth is, the God-man had a burning message to communicate during his sojourn on planet earth. This good news message was the theme of his life and ministry, from start to finish. He constantly harped on this same subject throughout his teaching. Yet somehow, despite our commitment to biblical truth, we evangelicals seem to have lost sight of Jesus' central message.

Opening message

How did Jesus begin his ministry? Matthew relates that his opening message ministry, was: *Repent, for the kingdom of heaven is near!* (chapter 4:17). Right from the start, Jesus was anxious to tell people good news about something called God's kingdom. Mark gives us a parallel version: *The time has come. The kingdom of God is near. Repent and believe the good news!* (see Mark 1:15).

While Matthew uses the term *kingdom of heaven*, the other gospel writers talk of the *kingdom of God*. Both terms refer to the same thing. Matthew was simply being sensitive to Jewish nervousness about using God's name in vain, and tended to substitute the word 'heaven'.

Sermon on the Mount

Next Matthew records for us Jesus' famous Sermon on the Mount, delivered in the open air to the disciples, with a large crowd eavesdropping.

How does the Sermon begin? 'Blessed are the poor in spirit, for theirs is the *kingdom of heaven.*' There's that phrase again. 'Blessed are those who are persecuted because of righteousness, for theirs is the *kingdom of heaven.* (Mt 5:3,10)

Jesus goes on to teach the crowd: 'This is how you should pray: "Our Father in heaven, hallowed be your name, your kingdom come, your will be done on earth as it is in heaven..."' (Mt 6:9,10)

Later in the same sermon, Jesus tells his listeners not to make a priority of food and clothing, but rather to 'seek first (the Father's) kingdom and his righteousness, and all these things will be given to you as well. (Mt 6:33)

This Kingdom of God is obviously a significant theme both of Jesus' opening declarations and also of the Sermon on the Mount.

Parables

Matthew then takes us on to the parables, stories of everyday objects and events told to communicate spiritual truths. Jesus is an astute story teller, and we can almost hear him thinking, 'Now, how can I best illustrate this truth?' But note the point of many of these parables. Jesus often begins with the phrase, 'The kingdom of heaven (or God) is like...'

By telling stories about the sower, the weeds, the mustard seed, the yeast, the hidden treasure, the valuable pearl, the fishing net, the vineyard workers, the wedding feast, and so on, Jesus explains truths about God's kingdom.

Great Commission

Barely a week before the crucifixion itself, Jesus makes another very significant reference to the kingdom. He is sitting with the disciples on the Mount of Olives, looking out over Jerusalem City with the temple rising above the city walls and gates. His disciples are agitated and confused. Jesus has just predicted the destruction of the very building which had inspired nationalistic pride and hope among the Jews. How could this be so? The Messiah surely was coming to restore Israel's glory, and to usher in a new Golden Age when the nations would come to Israel's light?! So they ask Jesus for signs of his coming and of the end of the age.

I can imagine Jesus shaking his head and saying, 'Guys, I know the sort of paperbacks you are reading - written by those sensationalist *apocalypticists* about end-time disasters. But my warning to you is this: don't preoccupy yourselves with such speculation. Yes, there will be wars, famines, persecutions and earthquakes. False messiahs will come and go. But watch out! Don't get sidetracked. Don't be deceived. Be on your guard. Only those who stay firm to the end will be saved.'

This is my paraphrase of the Olivet Discourse, recorded by Matthew, Mark and Luke, and which I suspect has often been misread as a sort-of Christian horoscope. I believe we can easily miss the main thrust of what Jesus is saying here. Rather than listing tell-tale signs of the End, Jesus explains that these hardships are merely birth pangs of the new era, and that the end is yet to come.

In Matthew's version (chapter 24:14), Jesus finally gives the one sign that must herald the end: 'this gospel of the kingdom will be preached in the whole world as a testimony to all the nations, and then the end will come.'

Here is the only place in the whole Bible where Jesus utters these words: *'and then the end will come.'* But what needs to happen first? The gospel of the kingdom has to be preached to all nations.

Final instructions

So not only does Jesus open his ministry talking about something called the *kingdom of God*. Not only is the *kingdom of God* a major theme of the Sermon on the Mount. Not only are most of the parables explaining truths about the *kingdom of God*. But now Jesus explains the Great Commission and the end times in terms of the *kingdom of God!*

And there's more.

After Jesus rises from the dead, he appears to his disciples over a period of forty days. What does Luke tell us he discussed with them? Why, of course, the *kingdom of God!* (Acts 1:3). Unfortunately Luke gives no clue as to the content of these talks. But it is very clear that Jesus considered this topic to be of utmost importance. It was his opening message, the theme of the Sermon on the Mount, the point of the parables, the heart of the Great Commission, and the subject of his final instructions.

During his ministry, in fact, Jesus spoke some 114 times about this *kingdom of God.* How often did he speak about the church? Surprisingly, Mark, Luke and John *never* record Jesus making any reference to the church at all! Only Matthew puts the word 'church' on Jesus' lips - a mere *two* times! (Matt. 16:18; 18:17)

What then can we conclude from this quick survey of Jesus' teaching and ministry? That Jesus is not interested in the church? No! He loves the church. He is the head of the church. He gave himself for it. He is coming back for his bride, the church.

But Jesus never told us to build the church, or even to make the church central in our lives. He said, *'You* seek the kingdom first, and *I'll* build my church.'

Now, I happen to believe in the local church, and in church planting. I have been actively promoting the DAWN church planting strategy and believe we need many thousands of new local churches across Europe.

But we need to recognise that, surprising as it may sound, the church was not the end focus of Jesus' ministry. Of course, he chose and trained the disciples, who became the pillars of the church. But he sent them out to witness to something called the kingdom of God. They were to share the gospel of the kingdom among all peoples. That was the focus of Jesus' ministry.

E. Stanley Jones, missionary statesman in India last century, once said,

If the kingdom of God was the central message of Jesus' ministry, then the rediscovery of the kingdom of God is the greatest human need.

Shalom

What then *is* the kingdom of God? And what are we praying for when we say, 'May your kingdom come'? What is the good news we are to take to all peoples before the end can come?

Our first clue comes from the opening chapter of the Bible, where we read the original instructions God gave to Adam and Eve: *be fruitful, multiply, fill the earth, subdue it, and rule over the fish, the birds and the animals.*

Here we learn something of God's original intention for this planet, and for the human race. He wanted his will to be done - on earth as it was in heaven. He wanted humans to be his regents to govern over the creation. Adam, Eve and their offspring were to be agents of his kingdom, his rule, his government. They were to ensure that God's *shalom* reigned - on earth as in heaven.

The Hebrew word *shalom* is far richer than the English 'peace'. It conveys the idea of everything being in right relationship and functioning as God originally intended - full, cosmic harmony.

This was God's original plan. But of course Adam and Eve's

choice to do things their own way produced terrible disaster - nothing short of cosmic alienation.

God however has not given up on his plan. Starting with Abraham, he begins to shape a creative minority through whom he will work to restore his government, his *shalom*, his kingdom.

The words kingdom, government, rule and *shalom* are closely related concepts. Isaiah foretold of the child who would one day shoulder the government, who would be called Everlasting Father, Prince of Peace, and that 'of the increase of his government and *shalom* there [would] be no end.' (Isaiah 9:7)

The prophet Daniel kept expectations alive of God's kingdom one day spreading throughout the whole earth (Daniel 2: 35,44). Daniel is sometimes called the prophet of the kingdom because of the recurring theme of the kingdom in his book, written in the den of paganism, Babylon. He tells the stirring story of how the world's most powerful ruler of the day, Nebuchadnezzar, was humbled to confess the God of Israel, the nation he himself had conquered, as the Most High God: 'His kingdom is an eternal kingdom; his kingdom endures from generation to generation' (Daniel 4:34).

Breakthrough!
So by the time we come to the New Testament, and the opening of Jesus' ministry, we already have picked up much understanding about God's kingdom: it is *universal, everlasting*, a rule of *righteousness*, the ultimate state of *shalom*. Briefly defined, the kingdom of God is where God's will is being done.

No wonder the crowds began to follow Jesus when he began to tell everyone everywhere that what the prophets had foretold was now on its way! God's kingdom was near! That was great news, something they had been waiting centuries to hear. Their forefathers had suffered under the Babylonians and the Persians. Two centuries earlier, the Greeks had desecrated the holy temple in Jerusalem with a statue of Zeus, provoking the Maccabean rebellion. And now they themselves lived under the yoke of the Roman occupiers.

Not only was Jesus merely talking about the coming rule of

God. People were being healed. Lepers were being cleansed. Blind people were seeing again. The demon-possessed were being freed. *Shalom* was breaking through! God's kingdom was already coming. God's will was being done in individual lives.

This was the evidence Jesus told John's disciples to take back to their master when they came with his question, 'Are you the one, or should we expect someone else?' (Luke 7:19)

This was indeed very good news.

Jesus instructed his disciples to spread this same good news of the kingdom. They too went out into the villages - and to their amazement demons obeyed their commands. They too saw healings! God's new order was breaking through - even before Jesus had gone to the cross!

Over the next three years, Jesus continued to demonstrate and to teach about life in God's kingdom. Much, however, seemed to go over the disciples' heads. And they were certainly a bewildered lot when all their hopes and dreams were crushed by the arrest, trial and execution of their master.

Loose ends

So when he appeared to them repeatedly after the resurrection, over a period of nearly six weeks, there were still many loose ends in their understanding.

'Master, is this the time you are going to restore the kingdom to Israel?' they asked on one occasion. The disciples had not yet grasped the big picture. They did not yet see that Israel had been chosen to be a blessing for all peoples, not for their own sakes. They probably had not at all registered what Jesus had told the crowd in the temple court just a few weeks earlier: that the kingdom of God would be taken away from Israel to be given to a people who would produce its fruit (Matthew 21:43).

They were still expecting Messiah to restore Israel's glory and zap her nasty enemies, starting with the Romans.

Had I been Jesus, I would have looked for the nearest brick wall to bash my head against - 'I've instructed them for three years, endured death by crucifixion, am about to leave the job to them to carry on, and still they understand *nothing?!?'*

Perhaps because of these huge gaps in their understanding, Jesus took this time to instruct them about the kingdom over these six weeks before the ascension. Maybe the reason Luke gives no hint of the content of these sessions is that Jesus perhaps gave them a recap of what he had already taught in his parables: that the kingdom would start small and grow slowly and in hidden ways; that the kingdom would grow side by side with evil in the world, like wheat growing among weeds; that the kingdom was the greatest treasure to be found and should be top priority for everyone; that, conversely, wrong priorites could strangle kingdom life - the cares of this world and especially the deceitfulness of wealth.

Jesus possibly reviewed the three easy-to-remember instructions about the kingdom, to be passed on to followers of all generations:

• *seek* God's kingdom first;
• *pray* for God's kingdom to come; and
• *share* this gospel of the kingdom with all peoples.

Chain reaction
When Jesus finally did leave the disciples, his last words mirrored God's first instructions to Adam and Eve: the disciples too were to spread out into all the world, spreading the good news of God's rule. They were to make disciples and teach them to do exactly the same, starting a chain reaction.

The difference was that this world was now a broken, sinful world. Yet the very movement these disciples were starting was to be God's rescue plan for an alienated world. Jesus' followers were called to be witnesses to God's *shalom* breaking into human affairs, to the advance of a new order of things. It would start slowly, but eventually would spread like leaven throughout the whole world. The events of Jesus' life, death and resurrection had confirmed that not even death could shake God's kingdom. Jesus was tougher than hell!

Later John would describe the final scenario in which '*the kingdom of this world has become the kingdom of our God and of his Christ*' (Rev 11:15). Paul would develop a theology for the early church in which history climaxed when God would reconcile all things under heaven and on earth to himself through his son Jesus (Col 1:20), producing God's *shalom*, when everything was restored back into right relationship, was the future.

Lost sight

This is the point at which, somewhere along the line, we lost sight of God's purposes. Just as Israel became ethno-centric, and forgot their broader calling, so we Christians have often become church-centred, and lost sight of our calling to be witnesses to God's new order, the kingdom.

God's plan is to reconcile *all things under heaven and on earth* under the lordship of Christ - the only thing left out of this category of 'all things' is hell!

His purpose is to see every area of life reconciled to his original intention: church and family, school and business, recreation and relationships, law and government, arts and entertainment, sport and healthcare, science and technology... you name it, it comes under the category of 'all things under heaven and on earth'.

The good news is that God has a purpose for every area of life, and we will live life to the full when we discover that purpose. This is a task for every believer in every walk of life, not just for an elite caste of 'priests'.

God has not abandoned his original purpose to see his kingdom come on earth, despite the major setback of the Fall. God's people, firstly in the Old Testament, and then in the New Testament, were to be his kingdom agents, witnesses to the new order, and agents of transformatio*n here on earth!* In teaching us to pray, 'May your kingdom come', Jesus was not referring to a heavenly reality; he was arousing our expectation that this is what God wanted for planet earth! The very next line of the prayer unfolds the meaning of the last line: 'May your will be done *on earth* as it is in heaven.'

Ask yourself: is it God's will for God's will to be done on earth? and in Europe? Is it God's will to reconcile all things under heaven and on earth to himself through Jesus?

If the answer is yes, then why in our churches do we concentrate on coming out of the world, getting saved, and going to heaven? Why is our ultimate focus on church programmes, church attendance figures, and the size of our congregations, when Jesus told us to seek God's kingdom first?

Shouldn't we be focussing on seeing God's kingdom come in greater and greater measure here on planet earth? here in Europe? Shouldn't we be concerned with the impact our congregation or cell of believers is having in transforming our neighbourhood or district? Shouldn't we be embracing our responsibility and role in being witnesses of the kingdom and agents of transformation, starting with the transformation of individual's hearts?

Personal salvation is of course essential. Jesus told Nicodemus that it was impossible even to enter God's kingdom without being born again (John 3: 3). But the end goal was not salvation - the goal was life in the kingdom! Why then have we whittled the gospel down to the message of salvation? That's merely the threshold.

The message that burned in Jesus' heart was not simply about getting saved. It was good news about living under God's rule.

The gospel Jesus proclaimed throughout his life and ministry was the gospel of the kingdom, not just the gospel of salvation.

To paraphrase the title of a popular movie: Yes indeed, *honey, we shrunk the gospel!*

Church & kingdom

But, I hear some say, are not the church and the kingdom the same thing? My answer is simply to try this test: substitute the word "church" for "kingdom" in the Lord's prayer, or any other verse. Are we to pray for God's church to come? Was it the good news of the church that Jesus went about preaching? Will the church of this world one day become the church of our God and of his Christ?! No, we simply cannot exchange these words without changing the meaning of the context.

What then is the relation between the church and the kingdom? We have already seen how Jesus sent his disciples -

the embryonic church - into the villages to witness to the good news of the coming of God's government, and to demonstrate its reality. God's people are called to witness to what they have seen and experienced of the rule of God in their own lives, and to demonstrate its power as they minister wholeness and healing, reconciliation and restoration. In their daily lives, God's people are to be agents extending God's *shalom* into every sphere of human life. Their aim is to *seek* God's kingdom first, to *pray* for God's kingdom to come, and to *share* the gospel of the kingdom with everyone everywhere.

Paul reminds the Ephesians that it is through the church that God displays his wisdom to the spiritual powers and principalities (Ephesians 3:10). God's people are kingdom agents. But the church is not the kingdom itself. The kingdom is where God's will is being done. Insofar as God's will is being done in our churches, there is the kingdom. But you and I know that that is not always the case in our churches.

Insofar as God's will is being done in other spheres of life - politics, education, law, etc, etc, so too is the kingdom advancing in these lifespheres.

Ideally the church should be a colony of the kingdom, a pilot project of the coming kingdom. Paul describes the role leadership gifts should play in the community of God's people as equipping the believers for their task out in the broader community (Ephesians 4:11).

But we have picked up much baggage over the centuries, accumulating many non-biblical ideas about church. Church has come to mean a building where formal ceremonies occur under the leadership of an elite clergy; where people hear about getting saved, going to heaven and being taken out of this world. Yet three whole centuries of the early church passed before a building was ever built for the purpose of Christian worship. Once however there were walls to hide behind, the concept of church changed. Instead of being in the world but not of the world, the church increasingly became of the world but not in the world.

So when we place the church central instead seeking the

kingdom first, we are guilty of doing what Israel did: we forget we are chosen to bless others, not simply to be blessed.

Already & not yet
Two thousand years have passed since Jesus declared the kingdom was near. What do we then make of the mess we see around us in the world at the start of the third millennium? Was Jesus' mission an heroic failure? Was it all a misunderstanding? Has the church failed in her mission?

Think back to the parable about the wheat and the tares; and the mustard seed; and the yeast. From small inauspicious beginnings, the kingdom would grow, and grow, and grow. Yet evil would also abound until harvest time.

As we look back over the twentieth century, we see the greatest century ever in terms of the expansion of the church–and the worst century ever in terms of man's inhumanity towards his fellow humans–this is the wheat and tares of Jesus' parable. As we enter the new century we can also expect to see continuing growth of God's kingdom, and increase of evil.

Yes, there is a sense in which the kingdom of God has already come, at least partially. God's will is being done in increasing numbers of believers on this globe.

Yet on the other hand, there is still much more to come. Obviously God's *shalom* has not yet been universally established. When the Berlin Wall came down, many hoped for a new reign of international harmony. Some talked of the 'end of history'. But names like Bosnia, Kosovo, the World Trade Centre and Bali have dispelled any such euphoria.

There is clearly a tension between the 'already' dimension of the kingdom and the 'not yet' dimension. How much can we expect the kingdom to come before Jesus returns? We know from what Jesus said that the good news of the kingdom must reach all peoples before he does return. But we also know from his parables that the tares in this world will not be dealt with until the final harvest.

That is not to discourage us from expecting ongoing

expansion of God's kingdom. It is clearly God's will. We are to pray for it. Just as none of us expect to achieve full Christlikeness in our present lives, we strive towards that goal.

So too we are to seek God's kingdom first, and strive towards the goal of seeing his *shalom* established on earth, as it is in heaven. That will require accepting a certain responsibility and fulfilling a certain role...

For discussion:

- Do you recognise these 'seven signs of hope' from your own experience? If so, give you own examples.
- How does your church or congregation view church planting? Has that perspective changed over the past ten years?
- Do you have any personal experience with African, Asian or Latin American believers? Which gifts do they bring to Europe?
- Is there a growing 'ecumenism of the heart' where you live? If so, why? If not, why not?

Where are the Christian people today
who see the status quo, who do not like what they see
who therefore refuse to come to terms with it,
who dream dreams of an alternative society
which would be more acceptable to God,
and who determine to do something about it?
John Stott[53]

8. Embrace!

... our responsibility and role

THE GOVERNOR OF SOUTHERN RUSSIA recently wrote a letter to the churches in his area (Orthodox, Baptist and Pentecostal) asking what contribution the churches could make to the betterment of Russian society. One denomination responded with a candid admission that they had little to offer. They were not preparing people for *this* world - but for the next.

What answer would our church or denomination give to such a letter?

The last action of Jacques Delors before his term of office expired as president of the European Commission, in 1992, was to write to religious leaders across Europe pleading for them to help recover the soul of Europe - to help shape her future.

My guess is that he is still waiting for a response from the evangelical sector.

In my travels around Europe I have encountered a wide spectrum of views among evangelicals concerning our responsibility for the state of our society.

In England, John Stott and others have been declaring for

---

53. John Stott, *Issues facing Christians today*, Marshalls, 1984, p.330-331

years the transforming power of the gospel and that God's purpose is for his people to be salt and light to the community making a difference.[54]

On the other hand, theologians from southern Europe have told me point-blank that the gospel is *not* about transformation, but about salvation.

In eastern Europe, to talk about Christian politicians or Christian businessmen is often akin to talk about frozen steam. Politics and business are seen as worldly activities unfit for God's people.

Kingdom agents

In the last chapter, we journeyed through Jesus' life and ministry to trace his central message - the Kingdom. Let's re-examine the task of God's People in Europe today, in the light of this message.

In Exodus 19:6, Israel was called to be a royal priesthood. In the New Testament, Peter applies this same concept to the new People of God (1 Peter 2:5).

So what is a *royal priesthood*, or a kingdom of priests? Part of the priestly role was to minister to God, and to intercede for the people. The other part was to bring God's word and absolution to the people. God's intention was to see his kingdom extended among the people, to see his will being done. His priests were his agents - *kingdom agents*, if you like.

James Bond, secret agent 007, was a (ficticious) kingdom agent on Her Majesty's service. His mission was to act in the interest of the queen (most of the time), to see her will being done. Being a royal priesthood involves being agents of God's kingdom, acting in God's interests to extend his rule, his kingdom, on planet earth.

Length, depth and breadth

When Jesus comissioned the disciples to spread the Gospel of the Kingdom, he suggested three dimensions in which this growth should happen.

---

54. E.g. Stott, 'Developing a Christian Impact on Society', Hope for Europe documenten, see: www.hfe.org/resources

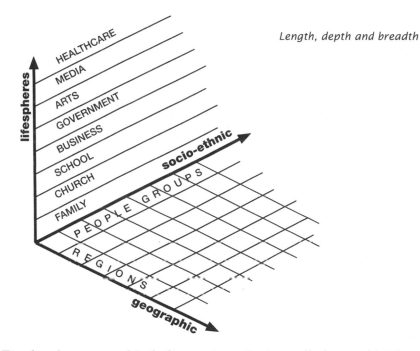

Length, depth and breadth

Firstly, the *geographical* dimension: *Go into all the world.* That means literally that God wants to extend his rule into every geographical part of this planet. We are to plant kingdom communities literally everywhere. A pressing question for us should be: *where are there few or no fellowships of believers in our city, country, continent and planet?*

Secondly, there is the *socio-ethnic* dimension: *Disciple all peoples.* That means the good news of God's rule needs to be transplanted into the cultures of all people groups everywhere. The Bible needs to be translated into all languages. Churches need to be formed everywhere in all manner of appropriate cultural expressions. The pertinent question is therefore: *which people groups have not yet heard the good news of the Kingdom in a culturally appropriate way - in our city, country, continent and planet?*

Thirdly, there is the *lifesphere* dimension: *Teach them to do everything I have commanded you to do.* In other words, *teach them to obey me in all things.* As we have seen from Colossians 1:20, Paul re-veals God's purpose to be the reconciliation of *all things* under heaven and on earth under Christ's headship. Every sphere of life is to be reclaimed for the Kingdom. No sphere under heaven and on earth is to be left outside the scope of the gospel.

No, the gospel is *not* just about personal salvation. Nor just about church activities. It has to do with the extension of God's rule, his will (being done in education, in government, in business, in the media, in the arts, in the entertainment world, in healthcare, in law... *in every human activity!* .

As kingdom agents, we have been given a mission to extend God's rule geographically, socio-ethnically and in every life-sphere. We can call this the length, the breadth and the depth of the Great Commission, as illustrated above.

Rebuilding
In the later stages of World War Two, as the allied forces punched their way up through France and the Low Countries towards the heart of nazi-Germany, a second 'army' was being assembled in England. The soldiers of this army were not armed with guns and bullets; they had been hand-picked for their skills and experience in local government or social services. They were former police chiefs, mayors, hospital administrators and civil servants. As soon as towns and cities were liberated, units of this second 'army' were moved in to rebuild the shattered infrastructure of the local communities.

To plant the flag and claim the territory as the paratroopers stormed their way through the frontlines in their drive towards Berlin was one thing. To begin the process of 'normalising' society, and rebuilding the community according the values of democracy instead of totalitarianism, was another.

Both were vitally necessary at the end of World War Two.

To plant the flag and claim territory for the Kingdom through evangelism and church planting is one thing. To begin the process of rebuilding the community according to the values of the Kingdom is another.

Both are vitally necessary at the start of Millennium Three.

Vocation

The word 'vocation' has come to mean a trade or a profession. It literally means 'calling'. The Oxford dictionary describes the word as a *feeling of being called by God to a certain career.* God doesn't just call people to be missionaries and pastors. He calls people into politics, into television work, into education, into business, into the arts, into medicine, into journalism, into making films, and so on, to be salt and light in all these spheres of life.

Jesus used these metaphors of salt and light when talking about Christian involvement in society. He used common everyday objects everyone understood. Yet somehow we still seem to miss the point.

Salt of course was used both for food flavouring and for preservation of meat. So when the food tastes saltless, whose fault is that? When the meat goes bad, whose fault it that?

When we enter a dark room, switch on the light and nothing happens, do we curse the room? Or do we realise something has gone wrong with the light?

So when we take stock of the situation in Europe today, who bears responsibility? We have to ask ourselves, what's gone wrong with the salt? What has happened to the light?

When Jacques Delors or the Russian governor ask for help from God's kingdom agents, what should they expect?

Reversal

Unfortunately, something happened over the past one hunded and fifty years to sideline evangelical Christians as serious players on the field. A one-sided pietism divorced the spiritual from the worldly, and the sacred from the secular. This in turn only encouraged widespread secularisation, as a comparision of the following two definitions reveals:

Secularisation: *that process by which society and culture has been freed from the decisive influence of religious ideas and institutions.*

Pietism: *that process by which society and culture has been freed from the decisive influence of religious ideas and institutions.*

Can you spot the difference? There was none!

This turnabout from the strong commitment to social and political involvement of eighteenth century evangelicalism on both sides of the Atlantic, for example, has been called the Great Reversal, referred to earlier.[55]

Various reasons have been suggested for this reversal, including evangelical reactions to theological liberalism and the social gospel, disillusionment and pessimism following World War One and the Great Depression, a gloom-and-doom eschatology, and a growing middle class conservatism and resistance to change among believers.

Thankfully a reversal of this Reversal itself has been underway over the past decades–particularly in 'off-shore Europe'–but its negative legacy still lives on among many continental Christians. The lack of a clear and strong evangelical voice in the European political arena is just one indication of this.

We need new resolve to embrace our responsibility and role for shaping Europe's future. We need a fresh understanding of our role as *kingdom agents*.

Transformed

One particularly moving scenario in J.R.R. Tolkien's *The Lord of the Rings* describes the transformation of Théoden, king of Rohan. The almost-messianic figure of Gandalf and his travelling companions arrive in the Golden Hall and are ushered into the presence of 'a man so bent with age that he seemed almost a dwarf....' At his feet 'sat a wizened figure of a man, with a pale wise face and heavy-lidded eyes.'

So we are introduced to the king and his counsellor, Wormtongue, whom we soon learn is in league with the enemy and has successfully crippled the king through whispered halftruths.

'I bid you come out before your doors and look abroad,' urges Gandalf of the king. 'Too long have you sat in shadows and trusted to twisted tales and crooked promptings.'

---

55. *See part two, chapter two*

Gandalf tells the king that age did not lie so heavily on his shoulders as some would have him think, and bids him cast aside the staff he was leaning on.

'He drew himself up, slowly, as a man that is stiff from long bending over some dull toil. Now tall and straight he stood, and his eyes were blue as he looked into the opening sky...'

Two of the king's men enter and stare in wonder at their lord, standing now proud and erect. Where was the old man whom they had left crouching in his chair or leaning on his stick?

As the king stretches forth his hand to grasp his long-disused sword, 'it seemed to the watchers that firmness and strength returned to his thin arm. Suddenly he lifted the blade and swung it shimmering and whistling in the air. Then he gave a great cry.'

Thus the king summoned his army and went forth to do battle.

What is the state of the church in our nation? Still bent and crouched, listening to Wormtongue's twisted tales? or standing tall and straight, reaching out to grasp her long-disused weaponry?

For discussion:

- How would our church or denomination answer the letter from the Russian governor?
- Discuss the three-dimensional diagramme *(the length, depth and breadth of the Great Commission)* in the light of your own town. In which districts, people groups or lifespheres is the Kingdom least advanced?
- Talk about the following: *'When we enter a dark room, switch on the light and nothing happens, do we curse the room? Or do we realise something has gone wrong with the light?*
- Give answers to the three questions at the end of this chapter..

The church we have known in the twentieth century
stands on the threshold of the future
much as a grain of wheat might stand before a ploughed field.
Gerard Kelly[56]

9. Transplant!

... the church into the 21ˢᵗ century

A LARGE WILLOW TREE USED TO DROOP OVER THE STREAM running down the side of our property. Where the trunk forked into two main branches, a split had been created by the storms of successive winters. Gale force winds finally forced the split open and one branch lay with its leaves on the ground, the other end connected to an ugly open scar on the other branch.

That, I thought, was the end of the tree. I called the council men who came and cut off the trunk about one metre from the ground and chopped up the branches for me to use as firewood. I expected they would return later to pull the stump out.

To my surprise, the council men planned to do nothing about the stump. It would, they informed me, simply grow its own new branches. I looked at the stump in disbelief, wondering how that sawn-off rump could produce new life.

However, as spring broke, lots of new whispy branches began to appear growing directly out of the stump, carrying green shoots and the promise of a new future. These new small

---

56. Gerard Kelly *Get a grip on the future without losing your hold on the past*, p.212

branches look nothing like the old majestic trunks. And the shape of the tree has been altered forever. But the spring green curly willow leaves unfurling on every square centimetre of these new branches are proof that new expressions of life are flowing out of the old stump.

That tree has become my backyard parable of hope concerning the twenty-first century church. A chorus of voices can be heard across Europe, from the mainstream to the margins, lamenting the current condition of the church and its unreadiness for the challenges of the new century. Some critics of the church have gleefully predicted the slow death of this 'anachronistic institution', come the new millennium. And indeed, the church as we have known it in Europe for many centuries may well be in the throes of a long-drawn out terminal sickness.

But as we began to suggest back in chapter six, there are signs that new shoots are emerging, that new expressions of church life are flowing out of the old stump. The shape of the twenty-first century church may be very different from what has preceded; but let us not underestimate the power for renewal latent in the old stump.

Candid

At the end of the nineties, church leaders in Holland gathered to take an honest look at the growing gap between the church and the surrounding culture. In a brave effort to hear from those outside the church, a panel of well-known personalities was invited to share with the gathered leaders their views on the church in Holland. Panelists included a television newsreader, the spokesperson for the Amsterdam police, leftist and green politicians, and a prominent homosexual columnist who during his brief and violently-aborted political career became one of Holland's most controversial public figures: Pim Fortuyn.

The atmosphere was electric as the three hundred almost totally male church leaders–from Reformed to Pentecostal–listened in rapt silence to candid views on the church as seen from the outside. Several spoke of their own church backgrounds in their youth, and of the process by which they stopped 'believing in Santa Claus'. For them, the church was simply irrelevant for life at the end of the twentieth century. Others expressed their wish that the church would be more open and inclusive, more integrated into the life of the community, more interested in what was going on in the rest of society.

I mischievously imagined the howls of derision that would have resulted had the chairperson asked the panelists' reactions to Moltmann's description of the church as 'an arrow sent out into the world to point to the future'.[57]

My wife (one of the few women present) and I sat there intrigued to be part of such a rare moment of honesty. As we broke into discussion groups, one minister in Romkje's group responded to the analysis that the church was irrelevant, by suggesting that maybe he should simply close his church down. Yes, agreed another, but what else were they trained to do?

That day could have been a watershed for many of those present. But, once back into daily routine, most would have continued on with business as usual, in the hope that yesterday's forms would suffice for tomorrow.

Former Baptist theology lecturer, Mike Riddell, is one however who has not been prepared to accept the status quo because he was not trained to do anything else. One of several voices from down-under calling for the reform of the church in the post-Christian west, Riddell believes the church itself to be the greatest barrier to the gospel in contemporary western culture.

> The forms of the church, its life and pronouncements; these act to prevent people from hearing the liberating story of Jesus. In the early days of the church's expansion through the Roman Empire, the cultural context was not unlike our own. Then, however, the church was regarded as new, fresh, exciting and revolutionary. Now, the church is seen as tired and reactionary[58]

---

57. *Jürgen Moltmann, Theology of hope, p.328*
58. *Michael Riddell, Threshold of the future, p.57*

Riddell teaches a university course on 'Church and Society' in which he asks his students to interview people with no connection to the church to share their impressions of it. 'Boring', 'irrelevant', 'a naive and behind-the-times club, where you are not supposed to have problems or to ask questions...' are typical responses the students regularly hear.

How have we allowed the community of Christ to gain such a reputation among onlookers? he asks.

Christianity has been smothered by churchianity, he answers, and before we can see what the new century should bring in terms of new expressions of life, we need to recognise the wretchedness and nakedness of our Laodicean churches today:

> For you say, 'I am rich, I have prospered, and I need nothing.' You do not realise that you are wretched, pitiable, poor, blind and naked. - Revelation 3:17

Only in recent years with the globalisation of the faith has it become apparent to western Christians how syncretised our church life has become, embracing many liberal western middle class values such as consumerism, individualism, careerism and security. Western Christianity, as viewed from those outside of the culture, is a Trojan horse, asserts Riddell.

Syncretism was always regarded as a problem for foreign mission fields, where traditional spiritual beliefs were interwoven with Christian values. Yet Protestant churches, and especially evangelical churches, have in Riddell's view become captive of the modern mind, deferring to the age of science, and adopting a scientific methodology in the study of the Bible. Even the expositional style of preaching which has defined Evangelicalism attempts to objectivise the text as an item for examination, reflecting the historic bias toward the mind as supreme arbiter of reality.

> Belief becomes a matter of mental assent, allowing us to go about our business in other areas of life, while resolutely claiming to be 'Bible-believing Christians'[59]

59. *Ibid, p.54*

156

John Drane of the University of Aberdeen is another who
believes the church has become a bulwark of modernist culture.

> Ironically, we Christians have talked and written more about the need
> for change and renewal during the second half of the twentieth century
> than at any other time in church history and, with one or two notable
> exceptions, it is hard to think of any previous comparable period when
> so little change has actually taken place. Our ways of being church at the
> start of the twenty-first century are virtually unchanged from what was
> going on in the nineteenth century.[60]

Drane applies the term *McDonaldization* to the contemporary
western church; that is, the 'destructive and dehumanizing
effects of social rationalization under the influence of modernist
thinking'.

Radical

If this is part of the problem, what might the solution be? What
might a twenty-first century church look like, then, breaking out
of the iron cage of modernity? To use another garden analogy,
what will be involved in transplanting the church into the
twenty-first century cultures of Europe?

To be honest, the picture is not yet really clear. But some
contours are emerging. Whatever the case, it calls for *radical*
change.

Does that mean throwing out all the old? Not necessarily. In a
time of transition, the old and the new will often exist together.
As a new road is under construction, traffic continues to flow
along the old path.

The Alpha movement already mentioned is a clear example of
this. Its origins were within the centuries-old Anglican church in
London, and yet has spread globally through all sorts of
denominations. Alpha was introduced in Holland by a
traditional Reformed mission agency. Both Anglican and
Reformed traditions were open for new radical models.

Let's examine this word, *radical*. From the Latin, *radix*,

---

60. Drane, *The McDonaldization of the church*, p.32

meaning root, *radical* implies returing to the roots. *Radicality*, as Riddell defines it, is the reclaiming and reinterpreting of tradition in such a way that it is consistent with the roots and yet adequate to the new situation.[61] What is needed for the twenty-first century are churches that will be consistent with Biblical roots, yet adequate to the new cultural and social environment.

Howard Snyder explains that the shape a wineskin takes depends on two factors. One, the properties of the wine inside; two, the atmospheric pressure from the outside. Wineskins for the new century thus will be shaped by the quality of the life of the Spirit, and the cultural context - not the traditions formed by past times.[62]

Here we should add a third factor: the suppleness of the leather itself. The question of appropriate structures flexible enough to respond to both the life of the Spirit and changes in the cultural environment is vital for the new century.

Recycled
Let us finish this chapter by noting insights of several who are attempting to peer into the future to see what the Spirit may be leading us towards in this new century.

Britain has experienced in recent years a strong revival of interest in Celtic spirituality - both Christian and pagan. While this resurgence has not affected mainland Europe to the same degree, the lessons being drawn are highly relevant.

John Finney, the Anglican bishop responsible for his denomination's Decade of Evangelisation in the nineties, wrote on the 1400th anniversary of the death of the Celtic saint Columba (d. 596), which coincided with the arrival of the Roman emissary Augustine of Canterbury. The merging of these two streams of Christianity gave birth to the mission movement which brought the gospel to the Germanic tribes in what is now the Netherlands and Germany.

Finney[63] drew the parallel between the task of these pioneer

---

61. see www.europ2004.org
62. See Howard Snyder, *The problem of wineskins.*
63. John Finney, *Recovering our past.*

missionaries among our pagan European ancestors and that of the church today. What did they do right then to attract a spiritually-aware polytheistic audience to faith in Jesus, God's Son? What can we learn from them today?

Roger Ellis and Chris Seaton also draw from Celtic well-springs as they too recognise 'some amazing parallels between the state of the Celtic world and our own, between the mission of the Celtic church and the church as it approaches the third millennium.'[64]

Finney, Ellis, Seaton and others point to the Celtic emphasis on community and relationships, mystery and symbolism, nature and environment, worship and creativity, lifestyle and celebration, mission and supernatural manifestations, as elements to be recycled in new expressions of the Christ movement.

The Celtic missionary movement was in some aspects a cell church movement. Bands of twelve would travel together to share the gospel and establish new communities. Whatever forms the future church must take, a return to a *koinonia*-centred expression of body life is essential.

William Beckham calls the cell church movement a Second Reformation in process.[65] This involves a major paradigm shift, not simply a matter of reorganising the traditional church into small groups, but rather viewing the congregation as the gathered cells.

Others like Wolfgang Simson see the return to the house church, meeting in private houses, as the way forward in the new century.[66]

Many of these elements fit well into models proposed by German church renewal advocate, Christian Schwartz who calls for yet a third reformation, following on from Luther's Reformation and the second Reformation of Pietism, a reformation that applies in practice insights from the previous

---

64. *Roger Ellis and Chris Seaton, The new Celts.*
65. *William A.Beckham,The second Reformation - reshaping the church for the 21st century.*
66. *Wolfgang Simson, Houses that change the world.*

reformations. 'The wonderful insights of Reformation and Pietism are largely smothered in the mire of unsuitable structures. In the third reformation we need to create structures which will be suitable vessels so that what the first two reformations demanded can be *put into practice.*[67]

James Thwaites, another voice from down-under, calls for a re-orientation from church-based activities and a focus on the congregation to a recognition that the daily work of the saints is the frontline of our engagement of postmodern society. These saints meet as church to be equipped for their daily task in the world.[68]

Experimentation

Much remains hazy as to what will emerge from this historic transition phase we are living through. What is clear is that we must make room for radical experimentation. Our old ways will not carry us into the the new century. We must allow younger leaders the freedom to experiment and make mistakes - and breakthroughs. Much is already happening on this front, with extensive use of the internet to link fledgling youth congregation movements across the continent. We mentioned in chapter six the *E-merge* gathering in Frankfurt in 2001 of adherents of several such networks, an event that would have frustrated older leaders who expect order and predictablility, but may have been just the sort of chaos out of which new order can emerge.

Another area where we need radical experimentation relates to post-Christian spirituality. A Swiss pastor from Lucerne told me that fully one third of the local population are into New Age. So he surfed New Age websites to see what sort of subjects interested them and organised events with titles like *Moments of Healing* and *Encounters with African Power.* He advertised these on website noticeboards, and booked meeting rooms in a neutral hotel venue. Sure enough, the room was filled with spiritual seekers. The pastor's African associate, dressed in colourful

---

67. *Christian A.Schwarz, Paradigm shift in the church, p.91*
68. *James Thwaites, The church beyond the congregation.*

traditional robes, was an evangelist who exercised a healing ministry. They both chatted conversationally with the audience, and moved around the room to pray for individuals, speaking out messages from a Higher Power. At the initial stage no overt Christian language was used. Yet healings were experienced and the seekers were powerfully aware of a transcendent presence. At a certain moment, the pastor announced that the source of this power people were experiencing was none other than Jesus of Nazareth, God's Son, and that He was present to meet those ready to do so. He invited people to respond then and there.

He is now accompanying over a hundred New Agers on a journey towards a greater understanding of the Greatest Mystery of the Universe.

Another Swiss pastor from a Salvation Army background, Danial Hari, advertised his book *Healing the Jesus way* in a New Age magazine together with an interview with him on the subject of healing. Hari claims that more than five hundred New Agers have ordered his book and have personally experienced God.

Does the Church have a future? Yes, but perhaps not without *radical* change. And only if we learn how to *work together!*

For discussion:

- What do your non-Christian friends say about the church in your country?
- What three factors determine the shape of the wineskin? What does that imply for the shape of the twenty-first century church?
- What factors have influenced the forms of the churches in your town?
- Why does Alpha fit the contemporary situation?
- Why could the Celtic missionary example be relevant for us today?
- Christian Schwartz appeals for a third reformation. What does he mean?
- With which examples of the 'emerging church' are you familiar?

The body is a unit,
though it is made up of many parts;
and though all its parts are many,
they form one body.
Paul (1 Cor.12:12)

10. Synergise!

... locally, nationally, regionally

A THOUSAND FACES FOCUSSED IN RAPT ATTENTION on the man with a handlebar moustache in the yellow shirt.

'The Masai of East Africa have a saying,' continued Ernie Addicott, a former missionary in East Africa, in his deliberate, resonant voice: 'If you want to travel fast, travel *alone*. But if you want to travel far, travel *together!*'

A murmur of consent rippled through the auditorium of spacious Budapest Congress Centre. The reason why the participants at HOPE.21 had converged on Hungary's capital from almost every European nation was expressed in the congress subtitle: *Shaping Europe's future – together!*

For four days in April 2002, they had been networking in a dozen hotels across the city. Each evening they came by bus, tram and metro to convene in the congress centre. While perhaps sounding pretentious, it was precisely to partner in the enormous challenge of helping to shape tomorrow's Europe that they had come together to learn from each other, to discover what work was already being undertaken and what more ought to be done.

Partnership across borders in the church, as noted earlier, had been notably lagging behind cooperation in politics, business, sports, media and even crime. Not only had there been a history of competition between denominations and traditions within nations, churches often had been conditioned over the years to hold a territorial mentality, hardly straying across national borders.

Now these thousand leaders had come to a working congress to help change all that. HOPE.21 was not to be an end in itself. It was to be part of a process, a growing movement rippling through evangelical circles and beyond, to encourage brothers and sisters to 'travel far by travelling together'.

Awkward

The process had its beginning in the late eighties, when a small group of leaders from various organisations began meeting on a regular basis. Stuart McAllister of Operation Mobilisation invited myself and several others from Youth for Christ, Campus Crusade, the Greater Europe Mission, the International Fellowship of Evangelical Students among others to explore ways to cooperate better in a fast-changing Europe.

To be honest, at first we felt a little awkward. Some were charismatic, others not. Some worked with Catholics, others would not. Some planted new fellowships, others did not. Quickly however we realised how small-minded such comparisons were in light of the enormous task we all faced in attempting to re-evangelise Europe.

When a few months later the Wall came down amidst global celebration, huge and rapid transformations were on their way. We no longer had the luxury of just 'doing our own thing'. We were entering an historic new phase of Europe's development. We had to work together.

So we called ourselves the *Coalition for the Evangelisation of Europe* (CEE), an informal relationally-based group that has continued to meet regularly ever since. Although there were bodies representing European evangelicals at the start of the nineties, none seemed able or willing to give a lead for a concerted and strategic response the dramatic events unfolding.

One or two conferences were called to explore the challenge of a New Europe, and wonderful-sounding declarations were drawn up. But something was still missing. Delegates would return home without a strategy for cooperative action.

Confused

Meanwhile, some significant new Anglo-American initiatives appeared on the continent, such as the DAWN church planting movement, *March for Jesus,* and the *AD2000 and Beyond Movement* (which rather optimistically aimed for world evangelisation by the end of the millennium). Each of these initiatives brought their own strengths, but the danger began to grow of a confused, crowded and competitive European landscape.

The *Coalition* proposed to bring all parties together around a Round Table, to strategize together for the future. The first Round Table was held in southern Germany in 1993. It aimed to build relationships and foster a climate of trust, respect and cooperation. Participants brainstormed together on the sort of ministry networks needed in Europe.

The following year at the Round Table in Prague, we agreed to create an umbrella framework for cooperative action, called *Hope for Europe.* Under this umbrella, networks began to take shape over the following years, stimulated by annual Round Tables held in various European cities. Each network decided on its own strategy and frequency of meeting.

As the new millennium drew near, we discussed at the Round Table the need for a large congress to unite leaders with a common vision of faith and hope for Europe's future. And so HOPE.21 was planned for 2002, in the now-centrally-located Budapest, and supported by the European Evangelical Alliance and the Lausanne Committee in Europe.

Puzzle

HOPE.21 had three ambitious goals: to build *networks across borders* in some 25 fields of work; to encourage *partnerships within each nation* among such fields; and to *nurture biblical hope and vision* for Europe's future.

Each evening in the Congress Centre, different groups of networks came to the podium with giant puzzle pieces representing their field. They placed the pieces on a map of a Europe shaped as one huge puzzle piece, waiting to find its place in today's world.

There were apologists and artists, broadcasters and business leaders, childrens' workers, church planters and those engaged in church renewal. City specialists, politicians, educationalists and evangelists mixed with those ministering among the disabled, families, women's and men's movements, as well as youth minstries. Others engaged in leadership development, relief and development, special prayer initiatives, reconciliation and worship.

Synergy
Now on the last morning, Ernie Addicott was challenging us all to travel *together,* to think partnership in our nations, and across borders in our networks.

'Working together has to do with one thing: *Synergy!'* continued Ernie.

'This is not just a buzzword used in business circles. It is also a biblical concept. It's the word Paul used literally in the Greek when he said that *all things work together* (sunergeo) *for the good of those who love God and have been called according to his purpose.* 'Paul refers to his fellow workers using the noun *sunergos* derived from the same verb *sunergeo.*

'Synergy is combined energy, united action, parts working together as a whole. One dictionary definition is: *the combined healthy action of every organ of a system.* This speaks of the Pauline imagery of body life, when the parts are properly related to each other. Together we can do far more than the sum total of our separate efforts.

'Synergy is also built into the very nature of the universe. One oft-cited example of synergy is the claim that one draft horse can pull two tons of weight - but two can pull twenty-tree tons! Nature is rich with examples of the amazing inter-relatedness of the cosmos.

'Ultimately the concept of synergy stems from the nature of the Godhead! The Father, Son and Holy Spirit model body life, operating in perfect harmony, perfect synergy.

'This is God's way of working. Psalm 133 says how blessed it is when brothers dwell together in unity.'

Awards

Earlier in the congress examples of 'synergy' had been recognised by the presentation of HOPE awards. Germany's YMCA, World Vision and the Evangelical Alliance were honoured for their creative partnership in conceiving and executing at Hannover's EXPO 2000 the *Pavilion of Hope*, a huge whale-shaped construction judged by the German public to be the best exhibition. The Albanian Evangelical Alliance also received a HOPE award for the united action of Albanian believers to extend warm and selfless hospitality towards the Moslem Kosovars fleeing before Milosevic's troops in 1999.

'Yes, there's a cost involved in time and effort invested in building relationships,' acknowledged Ernie, 'but its worth it! Jesus prayed in John 17 that we would be one just as he and the Father are one, so that the world might believe.

'We want Europe to have hope – to believe in Jesus the hope of the world. In that case, let us fulfil the prayer that Jesus prayed for us: that we may be one.

'If we want to bring hope to Europe, then we need to work together in unity – locally, nationally and across Europe,' Ernie urged.

'We have a long way to go to bring hope to Europe. So let's travel *together!*'

Orange cake

This challenge still resonated in our hearts as we dispersed from the main plenary hall, breaking up into national groupings in various halls and rooms of the congress centre.

Across from the Dutch delegation came laughter from the British. Next door were the Russians; further down the corridor were the Ukrainians, then the Bulgarians, and the Romanians.

The Spaniards and the Portuguese sat in circles in the aisles of the exhibition hall. The Croats gathered under the large stairways in the foyer. And so on, all addressing the same question: *how can we work together to help shape our own nation's future?*

At a dinner that evening, several national facilitators shared excitedly how that they had assumed they knew what God was doing in their country - until they began to hear the reports from their fellow-countrymen. God was up to far more than they had imagined, they admitted!

The Dutch, however, celebrated like none of the others. It happened to be *Koninginnedag*, Queen's Day, April 30. With orange cake (in honour of the royal House of Orange) and a rousing rendition of the national anthem, the ninety Dutch participants, representing organisations, churches, business, education and the political arena, reported from their various networks.

Many had made new relationships with others working in similar fields across borders. Some recognised how much they had to learn from other nations. Others had become newly aware of how much Holland had to offer other nations.

All were aware that the Holland they were returning to was a nation insecure about its own future. Pim Fortuyn had risen to controversial prominence by accusing the government of eight years of mismanagement in areas of immigration, multi-culturalism and welfare.

Turmoil

Days after the congress, the shocking news of Fortuyn's murder hit the headlines, unleashing even more questions about where Holland was headed. The memory of the panel he participated in with other well-known *Nederlanders* returned fresh to my mind. Had we, the evangelical movement in Holland, any real answers to the challenge they presented us that day, a challenge to engage effectively and become relevant to our society again?

This question also came from the mayor of Amsterdam, Job Cohen, when he met with evangelical leaders in the city. *What do you have to offer for a better Amsterdam?* he asked them, echoing the question from the governor of southern Russia. Here was a challenge needing responses not only from Amsterdam or Russia, but from Christians in every city and town in Europe.

The political turmoil that followed Fortuyn's premature death thrust a young new prime minister into the spotlight, Jan Peter Balkenende. Like the governor and the mayor, Balkendende also called citizens, particularly Christians, to help rebuild the social midfield, and for a relational rather than an individualistic ethos.

Not that Dutch Christians were totally passive on the social and political front, nor had nothing to say to a Job Cohen. Holland of all European countries has a particularly rich Christian political tradition, even if in recent years it has been accused of arrogance and being reactionary.

Reports from various sources indicated hopeful signs that believers were becoming more engaged, and were responding at the grass roots level to the challenge of Fortuyn and company. Christians gave six times as much as non-Christians to philanthropic causes. Workers in social welfare and caring activities were also disproportionately Christian. Christian initiatives responding to tensions in Holland's multi-cultural society were also low-key but widespread. A growing awareness and volunteer involvement of young people in social problems was emerging. In at least five cities in Holland, evangelical leaders had taken the initiative to ask local authorities what contribution they could make to the needs of the city.

Elements
Back in Holland, HOPE.21 participants met again and proposed a national congress to consider such questions, and to encourage *Hope for Europe*-type networks across Holland, linking people working in similar areas.

So HOOP.21 was planned for March 2004. It was to be a working congress modelled on the Budapest event, networking those across the nation working in similar fields, and encouraging cooperation between networks.

Each network was also requested to propose concrete answers

to the 'Cohen' question: *what can this network offer for a better Holland, at local or national level?* These responses were to be listed on the congress website as an inspirational inventory available to all.

The same three goals of HOPE.21 were now translated to the national level in HOOP.21: *national networks, local partnerships and vision for transformation.*

These three elements are embodied in the *Hope for Europe* logo on the cover of this book: a yellow star-cross on a dark blue background. It symbolises light shining in the darkness, a darkness that cannot overcome it (see John 1:5,6).

The star-cross intersection between the horizontal and the vertical represents the relational matrix *Hope for Europe* promotes at the European level: Europe-wide networks across borders, and partnership within nations among networks. The circle expresses the holistic vision of hope and faith bringing transformation to all areas of society, embracing all the fields of the networks and geographical regions

Applied at the national level in Holland, the symbol represents national networks (the horizontal), and partnership among networks at a local or regional level (the vertical).

On the last day of the national congress, participants met with others from their city or area to ask how they as 'people of hope' could influence each of the sectors of society depicted in the following diagramme. How could their churches and fellowships serve and contribute positively to the needs of the local community?

Paul in Ephesians 4:12 describes the task of church leadership as the equipping of the believers for 'works of service' or kingdom ministry. This should not be simply during church services, but in the outreach of the church to the world every day of the week, and into every life sphere.

A second chart proposed that the leadership in each church in a town or city identify and help equip those members of their congregation who could contribute to local emerging networks, e.g. in education, in the arts world, healthcare, working with families, youth, children and so on.

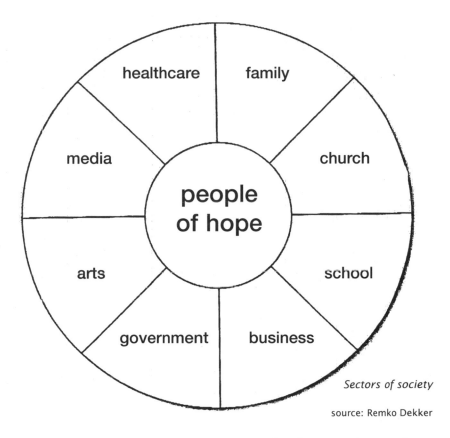

Sectors of society

source: Remko Dekker

In this way, all the churches in a locality can be working together to build networks for the various sectors of society.

Signs
Hopeful signs of such practical synergy are beginning to emerge. In Berlin, global symbol of division for forty years, one hundred and forty churches are working together with the goal of 'reaching all sectors of society with the gospel of Jesus Christ.' Under the umbrella of *Gemeinsam für Berlin (Together for Berlin)*,[69] they are promoting prayer forums and breakfasts for leaders, regional prayer groups and training, networks of professionals

---

69. see *www.gfberlin.de*

	Church 1	Church 2	Church 3	Church 4	.....	Church z	Total
Network 1	2	4	3	7		0	24
Network 2	1	3	12	2		2	36
Network 3	0	4	2	6		3	14
Etc							
Etc							
Network 21							etc
Etc							

source: Remko Dekker

and specialists in diverse areas, and a coordinating office for information and communication.

Axel Nehlsen and Hans-Peter Pache, two of the initiators, recognize that the 'worthy initiatives of the past often worked independently of each other. We cannot work in this way any more. Many of us are asking how we as Christians from different traditions can complement each other in order to fulfil our common calling.' These leaders see the need to recognize and affirm the whole body of Christ in the city, including traditional churches, mew emerging youth churches, cell churches, house churches and ethnic fellowships, and to fulfil their evangelistic and social responsibilities in the city together.

'Working together doesn't mean uniformity and compromise,' say Nielsen and Pache. 'It means unity in diversity. And when we build real relationships of openness and trust at the leadership level, we model unity to our fellowships.'

In Eskiltuna, Sweden, a Dutch evangelist Tjebbo van de Eijkoff invested seven years building synergy among the churches, the business community and the local government. After seven years the spiritual climate was radically changed. From having the highest criminality in the country, the city now had the lowest crime rate. Police from nearby Stockholm came to investigate what had caused the turnaround. Church members had become broadly involved in the community. Christians were seen as people who were working together to build a better future for their city. They were now being seen as *people of hope.*

Authority

The task of shaping Europe's future demands synergy in the Body of Christ - locally, nationally and across the whole continent. Europe is looking for models of unity with diversity. That's what the whole European Union experiment is about. Only when the People of God live and operate in synergy will we have the spiritual authority to disciple the nations of Europe in unity with diversity.

As individuals, as congregations, as denominations and as nations, we must learn how to complement each other's giftings.

As long as our adversary keeps us territorialised, competitive, divided through nationalistic thinking and denominationalistic thinking, we will be robbed of synergy and of spiritual authority.

Together we have been called to disciple the nations of Europe. Apart we cannot. God does not give the full picture to any one group. If we want to regain vision, faith and hope for tomorrow's Europe, we need to be in proper relationship with other parts of the Body of Christ.

We all can have a role in stimulating synergy in the Body, promoting unity and cooperation locally, nationally and regionally. We have not been called to do it alone!

We have been called to work *together* as people of hope.

For discussion:

- Discuss the concept of 'synergy' until everyone in the group understands it well.
- Read John 17 with each other, as a prayer for all the believers in your area. What would change if this prayer were to be fully answered?
- Explain to each the meaning of the vertical and horizontal elements in the *Hope for Europe* symbol.
- If Jesus was mayor of your town/city, what would he change?
- Are there already networks/partnerships/cooperative initiatives in your area? What models do you know of of cooperation between believers from different streams?
- Has there ever been dialogue between the Christian leaders and the mayor of your town/city about possible contribution towards a better community? If so, what was the outcome?

WE HAVE *come to the end of our journey -
through history's labyrinth in Part One
and through the ten imperatives of Part Two -
in our quest to recover hope and a future for Europe.*

DARE WE *now begin dreaming boldly about God's will for our town,
our country, our continent of Europe?*
DARE WE *be honest about the sins and mistakes in the church past
and present, rejecting the* Wormtongues *of pessimism and despair?*
DARE WE *remember what God has done in the past, and look to see
what God is up to today?*
DARE WE *allow the fullness of the gospel of the Kingdom
to radically change our lifestyle?*
DARE WE *embrace and accept our responsibility for the future of our
communities?*
DARE WE *be open for changes in the church consistent with her
biblical roots and at the same time relevant to twenty-first century
culture?*
DARE WE *we begin working together – locally, nationally and over
the borders – so that the church of Jesus Christ will be as 'an arrow
sent out into the world to point the way to the future'?*

IF SO, *then we will become known as* **people of hope.**

And whoever offers hope, leads.

A Millennium Creed:

OUR HOPE

We believe in the future!

We believe the best is yet to come!

Our hope is no mere optimistic wish or positive thinking.

Our hope is an anchor, sure and steadfast, unseen yet real.

The *ground* of our hope is the Triune Godhead:

The Revelation of the Father...
Whose *Person* is loving and faithful, merciful and gracious,
slow to anger, quick to forgive
Therefore we have hope!
Who *Plans* to give *his* people 'hope and a future',
to bless *all* peoples and fill the earth
with the knowledge of his glory
Therefore we have hope!
Who *Promises* to be with us always,
even to the ends of the earth
Therefore we have hope!

The Resurrection of the Son...
Who came to demonstrate the love of the Father
Therefore we have hope!
Who showed us how we should live to please the Father
Therefore we have hope!
Who defeated sin and death, reconciling us with the Father
Therefore we have hope!

The Reassurance of the Spirit...
Who came at Pentecost,
as promised by the prophet Joel
Therefore we have hope!
Whose fulfilment of that promise
promises the ultimate fulfilment
Therefore we have hope!
Who is the guarantee, deposit and foretaste
of what is yet to come
Therefore we have hope!

The *goal* of our hope is the Triune Godhead:

The Reign with the Father...
Who intends us to spend eternity with Him;
Therefore we have hope!
Who intends us to share in his divine nature,
to become like Him;
Therefore we have hope!
Who intends us to reign with Him as daughters and sons.
Therefore we have hope!

The Return of the Son...
Who, as before, will come again in time and space;
Therefore we have hope!
Who will consummate history,
breaking the cycle of hopelessness and despair;
Therefore we have hope!
And who will balance the books
and rule in justice and righteousness.
Therefore we have hope!

The Restoration through the Spirit...
Who, since Pentecost, has empowered
the global spread of God's kingdom;
Therefore we have hope!
Who, in the Twentieth Century, has inspired unprecedented
awakenings, surely making it the Century of the Spirit;
Therefore we have hope!
And, who promises further out pourings in the new Millennium
... until all peoples have been blessed.
Therefore we have hope!

Bibliography:

- Aikman, David *Hope, the heart's great quest,* Vine Books, 1995
- Balkenende, J. P., Kuiper, R., La Rivière, L. *De kunst van het leven,* Boekencentrum, 1999
- Balkenende, J.P. *Anders en beter,* Aspekt, 2002
- Bauckham, Richard & Hart, Trevor *Hope against hope,* Darton,Longman & Todd, 1999
- Beckham, W. A. *The second Reformation - reshaping the church for the 21ˢᵗ century,* Touch Publications, 1995
- Bjork, David *Unfamiliar paths,* WilliamCareyLibrary, 1997
- Bosch, David *Transforming mission,* Orbis, 1991
- Brueggemann, Walter *Living toward a vision,* UnitedChurchPress, 1982
- Brunner, Emil *Faith, hope and love,* Westminster, 1956
- Burnett, David *Dawning of the pagan moon,* MARC, 1991
- Cahill, Thomas *The gifts of the Jews,* Doubleday, 1999
  How the Irish saved civilization, Doubleday, 1998
  Sailing the wine-dark sea, Doubleday, 2003
- Catherwood, Sir Fred *Pro-Europe?* IVP, 1992
- Delden, J.E. *Uitgedaagd door de kloof,* Medema, 2000
- Dixon, Patrick *Futurewise,* HarperCollins, 1998
- Drane, John *The Bible phenomenon,* Lion, 1999
  What is the new age saying to the church? MarshallPickering, 1991.
  The McDonaldization of the church, Darton,Longman&Todd, 2000.
- Ellis, Roger & Seaton, Chris *The new Celts,* Kingsway, 1998
- Ellul, Jacques *Propaganda,* Vintage, 1965
- Finney, John *Recovering our past,* SPCK, 1996.
- Jenkins, Philip *The next Christendom,* Oxford, 2002
- Hall,Douglas John *The end of Christendom and the future of Christianity,* Trinity, 1997
- Hume, Basil *Remaking Europe,* SPCK, 1992
- Ignatieff, Michael *Virtual war - Kosovo and beyond,* Vintage, 2001
- Kaplan, Robert D. *The coming anarchy,* Vintage 2001
- Kelly, Gerard *Get a grip on the future without losing your hold on the past,* Monarch, 1999
- Knevel, A.G. *De boodschap en de kloof,* EO, 1997
- Korthals Altes, E, *Heart and soul for Europe,* Van Gorcum, 1999

- Lewis, Bernard *The crisis of Islam*, Weidenfeld&Nicolson, 2003
- Lewis, C.S. *Till we have faces*, HarcourtBrace, 1984
- van der Linde, J. M. *De wereld heeft toekomst*, Kok, 1979
- Meddeb, Abdelwahab *Islam and its discontents*, Heinemann, 2003
- Moberg, David O. *The great reversal*, Scripture Union, 1972
- Murray, Iain H. *The Puritan hope*, Banner of Truth, 1971,
- Newbigin, Lesslie *The Gospel in a pluralistic society*, SPCK, 1989.
- Pasley, Ben *Enter the worship circle*, Relevant, 2001
- Peck, M. Scott *In search of stones*, Simon & Schuster, 1995
- Postman, Neil *Amusing ourselves to death*, Penguin, 1985
- Riddell, Michael *Threshold of the future*, SPCK, 1998
- Sacks, Jonathan *The politics of hope*, Jonathan Cape, 1997
  Faith in the future, Darton, Longman & Todd, 1995
  The dignity of difference, Continuum, 2002
- Schaeffer, Francis A. *He is there and he is not silent*, Tyndale, 1972.
- Schirrmacher, Thomas *Hope for Europe, 66 theses*, 2002
- Schluter, Michael & Lee, David *The R Factor*, Hodder&Stoughton, 1993
- Schluter, Michael & Lee, David *The R Option*, RelationshipsFoundation, 2003
- Schwarz, Christian A. *Paradigm shift in the church*, ChurchSmart Resources, 1999
- Simson, Wolfgang *Houses that change the world*, Paternoster, 2001
- Sine, Tom *Mustard seed versus McWorld*, Baker, 1999
- Stott, John *Issues facing Christians today*, Marshalls, 1984
- Tutu, Desmond G, *No future without fogiveness*, Random House, 1999
- Thwaites, James *The church beyond the congregation*, Paternoster, 1999
- Walker, Andrew *Telling the story*, SPCK, 1996
- Wessels, Anton *Europe: Was it ever really Christian?*, SCM, 1994

Websites:
_____

General information about Europe:
www.euobserver.com
General news about the EU.
www.euprayer.com
Prayer information about the EU.
www.europa.eu.int/comm/cdp/scenario/index_en.htm
Scenarios of Europe in 2010
www.europeanvalues.nl & www.uvt.nl/web/fsw/evs/EVSN/frame.htm,
The European Values survey is a major sociological project researching how
important Christian values still are in Europe and what coherent alternatives
there may be. This site is a slide show with comparative graphics showing
information for each European country concerning belief in God, religion,
church attendance etc. See also www.worldvaluessurvey.org

Christian cooperation, Europe:
www.hfe.org
The *Hope for Europe* website with many resources and links to other websites
about Europe; also the *HfE* story; a report with photos and videoclips on the
HOPE.21 congress in Budapest, 2002; information about *HfE* networks with
articles, news, events, activities, bookreviews, documents and declarations.
www.gfberlin.de/english/index.html
Gemeinsam für Berlin e.V. is an initiative in Greater Berlin with the goal
reaching all sectors of society with the gospel of Jesus Christ.
www.europ2004.org & www.samenvooreuropa.nl
Making visible the richness of Christian life in Europe.
www.hoop21.nl
(Dutch only) Information about the prayer- and work-congress on shaping
Holland's future together, sponsored by the Dutch EA and the EZA
(Evangelical Missionary Alliance).

Reconciliation initiatives:
www.relationshipsfoundation.org
The Relationships Foundation, with Dr Michael Schluter, Cambridge, UK
www.reconcile.org
The International Reconciliation Coalition with John Dawson.
www.recwalk.net .
Reconciliation along the Crusader trail, with Lynn Green.
www.lifelineexpedition.co.uk
Reconciliation in relation to slavery, with David Pott

New initiatives in the church
www.alphacourse.org
About the fast-growing Alpha movement worldwide.
www.emergingchurch.org & www.alternativeworship.org
About models of the church and of worship for the 21st century.

Examples of initiatives among New Agers:
www.daniel-hari.ch

Weekly Word:
Jeff Fountain writes a weekly English language column, about various
current themes, particularly concerning Europe.
Past ww's can be viewed and downloaded at:
www.ywameurope.org/news/word.asp
To subscribe to receive these weekly, send a blank email to:
weeklyword-subscribe@list.ywameurope.org

*Jeff Fountain has lived in Heerde,
the Netherlands, since 1975
and with his wife Romkje has three adult sons.
After completing history studies at
Auckland University, New Zealand,
he worked as a journalist,
and later as travelling secretary
for IFES in his homeland.
He and his wife were leaders
of the Heidebeek training centre and community
of Youth With A Mission from 1980 to 1993.
In 1990, Jeff became the regional director
of YWAM Europe.
Jeff was an initiator
of the Hope for Europe movement,
and of the HOPE.21 congress
in Budapest, 2002.*

*May the God of hope fill you with joy and peace
and may the power of the Holy Spirit fill you with hope!*

Rom.15:13

Notes

Notes